THE
RELAY

THE RELAY

PASSING ALONG YOUR FAITH
IN THE RACE TO SAVE CHRISTIANITY
FROM EXTINCTION

George Shamblin

Union Hill Publishing
200 Union Hill Drive, Suite 200
Birmingham, AL 35209

www.georgeshamblin.com

1 2 3 4 5 6 7 8 9 10

Printed in the United States of America

To my wife Jill:
my best little friend in the whole wide world.

To my daughter, Sydney, for dedicating three summers
to help me see this through.

Table of Contents

PRELIMINARIES   1

1. ADAM
   The First Runner, the First Failure   17

2. MOSES
   Indeed, It Is Your Life!   32

3. JOSHUA
   This Book Shall Not Depart From Your Mouth   48

4. DAVID
   The Paper Chase   63

5. JOSIAH
   What Went So Terribly Wrong?   81

6. JESUS
   The Words You Placed in My Hands, I Have
   Placed in their Hands   97

7. JOHN
   The Apostle of the Word   113

8. PETER
   On Your Mark, GO! Get Set   127

9. PAUL
God's Power Perfected through Our Weakness   144

10. HEBREWS
Hitting the Wall   162

THE PODIUM   179

PRELIMINARIES

It was the Summer Olympics of 1968 in Mexico City. The final event, the marathon, took place on one of the hottest evenings on record. At nearly 7,400 feet above sea level, the air in Mexico City provides one-third less oxygen than the air at sea level. The heat and elevation created a formidable challenge for the competitors, so severe that 18 of the 74 participants were unable to finish.

Early on, Tanzanian runner John Stephen Akhwari was slowed by severe cramps. Determined to work his way back toward the front of the pack, he jockeyed among a few runners, tripped, and was trampled by others who were following behind. As a result, Akhwari suffered a badly gashed and dislocated knee, a blow to the head and a bruised shoulder. After having his knee quickly bandaged by trackside medics, the Tanzanian elected to finish the second half of the race despite being repeatedly asked by officials to stop running.

An hour after Mamo Wolde crossed the finish line claiming gold, Akhwari hobbled to a distant last place. The closing ceremonies had just ended, and spectators began to gather their belongings and leave the arena. When all but a few people had gone home for the night, a lone runner wearing the colors of Tanzania could be seen making his way toward the Olympic Stadium. Bloody and bruised, Akhwari limped past the finish line to receive a last-place standing in the race.

When later asked by a reporter why he had subjected his severely injured body to a tremendous amount of pain rather than dropping out of the race, Akhwari responded: "My country did not send me to start the race. They sent me to finish."

Within each epoch of history, among every people group on Earth and across all mother tongues, a select handful of words are so universally understood that nothing more than hand gestures are needed to translate their meaning. For instance, take the word 'running' as illustrated in Akhwari's story above. Regardless of dialect or pronunciation, when we read or hear the word 'running,' a universal chord is struck in us, causing, without reason or without warning, an instinctive urge to go. Not sure where to, nor how far, but something beyond us exists out there summoning us to get there quickly, and the urgency for doing so cannot be explained.

It would only stand to reason that the One who came up with running in the first place would draw from a limitless storehouse of running analogies and metaphors when drafting His hand-inscribed letters to us from Home. God's unblemished design for The Old and New Testaments was this: Of all the readily available analogies and word pictures with which to compare and contrast the godly life, the Bible's 40-

 The long-distance relay is the single most fitting analogy for the Kingdom of God and those who play their part in it—a succession of runners passing a single baton over time, from generation to generation to generation.

plus authors writing over the course of 1,500 years used running more than any other—an astonishing 250 times. From antiquity to modern times, we find a sacred common ground on which all can relate—running.

In no way does this mean all running analogies about faith are equal or right. There's an increasingly popular mantra, "Christianity isn't a sprint, it's a marathon"—and no worse analogy could be found. Sprints and marathons remain individual events. One of them just happens to be longer than the other. Rugged individualism may be a uniquely American trait, but it is certainly not Biblical. Additionally, what happens after an individual's race is run? What about the rest of our race?

In any given region, Christianity is never more than one generation away from extinction. Need proof? Scripture's pages are littered with stories of entire generations either falling away from the faith or forgetting their God:

- *"Help, LORD, for the Godly man ceases to be, for the faithful disappear from among the sons of men."* (Psalm 12:1)

- *"The Godly person has perished from the land, and there is no upright person among men."* (Micah 7:2)

- The most glaring example can be seen with the multitudes who *"served the Lord all the days of Joshua."* (Judges 2:7) Once they finished their races of faith, if you will, and were *"gathered to their fathers, there arose another generation after them who did not serve the Lord, nor yet the work which He had done for Israel."* (Judges 2:10) Scripture rarely strings together more sobering words.

Christianity is no sprint. Christianity is not a marathon.

To what type of race, then, should we liken it? The long-distance relay is the single most fitting analogy for the Kingdom of God and those who play their part in it—a succession of runners passing a single baton over time, from generation to generation to generation.

Which of the following might apply to you?

- I recently wrapped up a 50-hour work week only to realize just how few minutes I logged for telling my Christian story.

- My faith could be best described as public on Sunday but private Monday through Saturday.

- I take in far more truths about Christianity than I regularly give out.

- Outside my immediate family, it would be easy to count the number of people I evangelized over the last month.

Each of these statements describe what a spiritual sprinter or a spiritual marathoner looks like—and neither is what God called you to be.

God the Father created you for a greater purpose. He called you to not only follow His Son Jesus, but to go and invite others to *"come and see for yourself."* (John 1:46) Christianity's vitality and endurance relies on us sharing our faith with others, both

---

The long-distance relay is the single most fitting analogy for the Kingdom of God and those who play their part in it—a succession of runners passing a single baton over time, from generation to generation to generation.

---

in the here and now and with future generations. You've received the faith from those around you and before you; now you need to pick up the baton and share your faith with others.

Do you want your generation to be remembered as the one that dropped the baton? Do you want to be known as someone who kept the faith all to yourself, as someone who ran a solitary race without the consideration of others? If your greatest joy is found in Christ, wouldn't it be wrong to keep that joy all to yourself? What would it feel like for your children, your grandchildren or even complete strangers to ask, "Why didn't you tell us about the goodness of the Lord? Why didn't you share with us who He is and how we might know Him? Why did you remain silent?"

If you feel this is the time for you to make a bold switch and you're prepared to make the transition, this book will coach you through the process. It will give you food for thought and fuel for action. *The Relay* will inspire you to become bolder in telling your story so you can best minister to others. Each day can start on new footing: "I will share Christ with one person before the sun goes down."

Don't be surprised to find yourself engaged in more conversations over spiritual matters. As you learn how to share Jesus, you'll discover more and more opportunities to do so. By the end of Chapter 11, you will become a relay runner, no longer a solo competitor.

Jesus' commission for us was never to merely start the race but to finish—and, in the process, to win as many others for

Him along the way. Or, as an earliest convert saw it: becoming *"all things to all men, so that I may by all means save some."* (I Corinthians 9:22) Just as a race only becomes a relay when a changeover occurs—i.e., the exchange of the baton from one runner to the next—Christianity only remains "Christian" as long as continual changeover takes place, a constant passing over of the baton from one believer to the next. Or, as the Bible literally states: *"an exchanging of the hands."* That is the entire premise of *The Relay* in one word: **Changeover!**

To the Christian who is "in" as well as the seeker who is close, your own faith adventure serves as the perfect case in point. How did you get where you are the way you did?

Perhaps you chased hard after Christ long before the first spiritual seed took root in your body. Others extended the baton for you to take hold of and blazed a path for you to follow—you can recount them by name. But what about the host of lesser-knowns? Sunday school teachers, coaches, dormmates and others with scabs as proof of oft-bent knees. Or that one kind soul whose name presently escapes you, the only one who stopped to lift you up as the rest of the pack ran right by. *"Woe to the one who falls when there is not another to lift him up."* (Ecclesiastes 4:10) Not to mention the significant contribution of all those who clapped and cheered.

And there are more, so many more just below the surface, too innumerable to count. Imagine your spiritual life in pictures—vintage Polaroid photos, let's say, the ones with tabs allowing you to peel apart the positives and negatives. As the outer film is peeled back ever so slightly, previously blurred faces from among the crowd start to emerge, becoming so numerous that an ancient Olympic stadium couldn't hold their ranks.

The realization strikes you: Each one ran the relay ahead of you and played a part in passing you the baton, recalling to mind that familiar refrain: *"therefore, since we have so great a cloud of witnesses surrounding us, let us also lay aside every encumbrance and the sin which so easily entangles us, and let us run with endurance the race that is set before us, fixing our eyes on Jesus, the author and perfecter of faith."* (Hebrews 12:1-2)

Don't worry, your time for extending the faith to others will come soon enough. But for now, to continue in the spirit of the relay analogy, let's take a minute to walk through four essentials you'll need to understand before you enter the race. Each is meant to prepare you for the chapters ahead, to set a steady pace and get you on your way.

The Baton is the Word of God

The phrase "passing the baton" goes all the way back to the inaugural Olympics in 776 BC. Relay teams were established where each member passed a hollow cylinder to succeeding runners—and track teams have been doing the same ever since. When reading *The Relay,* you'll quickly discover a host of the Bible's faithful passing off one baton in particular, which is the very Word of God. It's as if each Biblical character conveys a common refrain to successive runners—even to you and me—that says, "If I could only hand off one baton to you, just one baton that not only contains the words of life but in every sense **is** your life, it would be the Word of God."

All of history's saints are interconnected by the passing of a single baton over time: the Holy Scriptures. And so it only stands to reason that the Bible alone will outlive all else: *"Heaven and earth will pass away, but My words will not pass away."* (Luke 21:33)

The Word is Meant for Movement

"No reserve. No regret. No retreat." That is the postscript to William Borden's life, cut short en route to spreading the

Word in China. He realized that just like a baton, the Writings of God were designed for movement.

The Bible personifies itself as moving: *"His word runs very swiftly."* (Psalm 147:15) This depiction of God's Word running wasn't lost on an astute theologian such as the Apostle Paul. *"Finally, brethren, pray for us that the Word of the Lord will spread rapidly (literally, "run" rapidly) and be glorified, just as it did also with you."* (II Thessalonians 3:1)

Paul used the Greek word *trexo*, from which we get our English 'trek.' *Trexo* meant so much more than taking a long hike. In Biblical usage it implied extreme intensity, literally "to run wide-open with full effort and directed purpose" like an ancient Greek athlete advancing speedily with an "intense desire to get to the goal as quickly as possible." Paul, according to theologian Leon Morris, "is not looking for a single striking manifestation of the Word, but for its continuous swift advance and its continuing arousing of admiration."

Furthermore, the necessity of ongoing Gospel motion is evident in Jesus' firm command (not suggestion) in Mark 16:15: *"Go into all the world and preach the Gospel!"*

'Go' precisely means "to transport or transfer something from one destination (port) to another." Saint Peter did exactly this when preaching history's first Christian sermon. As Acts 1:16-17 describes, no sooner had Peter stood than the transfer began: *"Peter stood up in the midst of the brethren and said, Brethren, the Scripture had to be fulfilled . . ."*

Of all the mediums God could have chosen to transport or transfer His message to Earth's four corners, the choice was clear: He chose humans. Which means that for His devotees, idleness is not an option. The greatest travesty would be for anyone to bind that which was meant to run. For the faith to abound, which is no different than for a relay to abound, The Good Word given to us must, in turn, be given out. The messenger with his message and the runner with his baton were both made for motion. It is imperative they keep going.

"On Earth we are wayfarers, always on the go. This means that we have to keep on moving forward. Therefore, be always unhappy about where you are if you want to reach where you are not. If you are pleased with what you are, you have stopped already. If you say, 'it is enough,' you are lost. Keep on walking, moving forward, trying for the goal." —St. Augustine of Hippo

You Are Not the First Runner

The Bible is laden with stories of those who've carried the baton before us, who've stumbled, who've persevered. The specifics of *The Relay* will soon follow, but for now, let's keep our eyes on the bigger picture with previews of the next 11 chapters.

CHAPTER 1: ADAM The world's first runner, the first failure, dropped the baton right out of the gate. The Relay seemed over before it could start. Ours, however, is the God of second chances; The Relay would continue, the games had to go on.

CHAPTER 2: MOSES If but one runner typifies The Relay it would be Moses, who ran for the better part of 120 years. But he could only go so far. The last leg through the River Jordan would be led by another; his mentee Joshua had been waiting in the wings. At long last, God's people Israel would finally come home.

CHAPTER 3: JOSHUA His inaugural sermon in the Promised Land picked up where Moses left off, albeit on the opposite side of the Jordan. His message commenced with these familiar words: *"Remember the Word which Moses the servant of the Lord commanded!"*

CHAPTER 4: DAVID Israel's most relatable king openly shared his setbacks among successes, his tragedies among triumphs, leaving the impression that he wrote largely with you and me in mind.

CHAPTER 5: JOSIAH Before his reign, "the people of God were asleep. Only a loud voice would awaken them from their slumber." His would become that voice, upending the entirety of nations that had long since forgotten their God and who did not know His Word.

CHAPTER 6: JESUS The New Testament never mentions anything about Jesus running, much less participating in a relay. He cannot be relegated as One among many. This does not, however, mean He carried out all of His Father's will to the exclusion of others. In fact, quite the opposite. It would be His followers who took the race to a whole new level and a whole new arena. The goal was not to win a race, but to win the world.

CHAPTER 7: JOHN The self-designated "disciple whom Jesus loved," the sole person to peer beyond the finish line and prepare us for what must soon take place.

CHAPTER 8: PETER A former fisherman turned evangelist, a real "On your mark! Go! Get set!" kind of guy. His habit was to take off minus the baton—forget the handoff; he just ran. After countless false starts, slips and blunders, he eventually hit full stride.

CHAPTER 9: PAUL His faith journey began while traveling to persecute Christ-followers on an obscure Damascus road and continued until the final lap. Christianity's most unlikely convert reminds us that through our weaknesses God's strength most gloriously shines.

CHAPTER 10: HEBREWS This author knew well what it meant to "hit the wall" and still endure, not to mention the power of a cheering crowd: *"therefore, since we have such a massive assembly of martyrs surrounding us . . . let us run with endurance the race that is set before us."*

CONCLUSION: THE PODIUM What it means to break the tape and know *"I have fought the good fight, I have finished the course, I have kept the faith; in the future there is laid up for me the crown of righteousness, which the Lord, the righteous Judge, will award to me on that day."* (II Timothy 4:7-8)

The End Game: Winning More Followers

As we've seen, this passing of the baton in an age-old relay has and will endure until the *"Gospel of the Kingdom shall be preached in the whole world as a testimony to all the nations, and then the **end** will come."* (Matthew 24:14) The Greek word Jesus used for 'end' means "the last in a succession or series, that by which a thing is finished, its close." According to plan, the end or last in a succession or series will culminate at a specified juncture that He ordained before time.

But until the very end, much work remains to be done. There's a race not only to be run, there's a race to be won. As the Apostle Paul stated: *"Do you not know that those who run in a race all run, but only one receives the prize? Run in such a way that you may win. Everyone who competes in the games exercises self-control in all things. They then do it to receive a perishable wreath, but we an imperishable."* (I Corinthians 9:24-25)

When describing exactly how we must run to win, Paul selected a surprisingly violent Greek word for winning, *katalambano,* which means "to hunt down, to aggressively seize." This means that we as Christians are to run aggressively, not to place but to win at all costs.

Unlike Emperor Nero who, in the 67 AD Olympics was awarded 1,808 prizes by paying off the judges, the New Testament positions a victor's wreath just beyond reach, which for the Christian is of such immense value that to forfeit one's all in its pursuit would be well worth the price. Before his martyrdom, missionary Jim Elliott left us with this ageless perspective: "He is no fool who gives what he cannot keep to gain that which he cannot lose."

To ultimately win as God purposed His people to win means to cross the finish line not alone, but rather linked arm-in-arm with the multitudes whom we introduced to Christ. In other words, to finish as a relay runner, not a sprinter or marathoner.

Countless converts are ready to be won right now. The ever-expanding Kingdom of God is marching on with or without you. Therefore, heed Will Rogers' words: "Even if you're on the right track, you'll get run over if you just sit there." Simply put, it's time you get a move on.

What This Book Means for You

So, the questions become, "Why was *The Relay* written? What is its intent or purpose for me?"

First and foremost, an alarming contradiction has become increasingly evident to me for years: On one hand, Jesus routinely drew attention to the fact that *"the harvest is plentiful, but the laborers are few; therefore beseech the Lord of the harvest to send out laborers into His harvest!"* (Luke 10:2) And yet we live in a culture that not only gave birth to the "Christianity is a marathon" mindset, but continues to bless and promote it. The sad result: laborers overly concerned with self, not the harvest.

If, in some small way, *The Relay* propels individuals who are running for self into team members running for others, or if it propels sprinters and marathoners into becoming long-distance relayers, then my purpose in writing will be complete.

To that end, I am targeting three talent pools from which I'd have no greater joy than to see The Lord of the Harvest recruit. Three talent pools that would *"beseech The Lord of the Harvest to send out laborers into His harvest."* They are the Christian with stagnated pace, the spectator sitting in the stands and the Christian currently running strong.

For Christians Who've Slowed Their Pace

I hope to spur you to the second greatest day of your life, which is the day you lead another to Jesus (the greatest being the day you came to know Him). Experiencing this second greatest day of your life will allow you to recapture the fervency with which you previously ran.

"You never go away from us, yet we have difficulty in returning to You. Come, Lord, stir us up and call us back. Kindle and seize us. Be our fire and our sweetness. Let us love. Let us run." —St. Augustine of Hippo

For Those Sitting Idly in the Stands

I'd like to wave you out onto the track, that you might know Christ and Him crucified, and run with higher meaning as significance has its place.

"It is not the critic who counts; not the man who points out how the strong man stumbled or where the doer of deeds could have done them better. The credit belongs to the man who is actually in the arena; whose face is marred by dust and sweat and blood; who strives valiantly. Who errs and comes short again and again; who knows the great enthusiasms, the great devotions. Who spends himself in a worthy cause. Who at the best knows in the end the triumph of high achievement; and who at the worst, if he fails, at least fails while daring greatly so that his place will never be with those timid souls who know neither victory nor defeat." —Theodore Roosevelt

For Christians Currently Running Strong

My hope is that your path might shine the brighter past first dawn. (Proverbs 4:18 — *"the path of the righteous is like the light of dawn, that shines brighter and brighter until the full day."*) With so many to win in such a short time, we request that you please excel still more.

> "If you run, you are a runner. It doesn't matter how fast or how far. It doesn't matter if today is your first day or if you've been running for twenty years. There is no test to pass, no license to earn, no membership card to get. You just run." —John Bingham

There's a tough race ahead. I trust you'll do well. But for the moment, allow me to extend an image for you to keep handy, like a reservoir of water stored for future use. Draw from it as you may so you can persevere, so you can endure.

Imagine for a moment that your palm is forged with that final saint's palm around the baton, which is the Word of God. An initially faint yet resounding blare of the trumpet calls from the east (Joel 2:1), inviting all mankind to assemble upon His Holy mountain in Jerusalem. You stand overcome with the realization that this is it; it's actually here; your pass of the baton was the last Earth will ever see; the age-old relay has come to its close, and the end of all things has been ushered in.

Then, as the Heavenly host holds its breath in earnest expectation—anticipating The Lion of Judah's final congratulatory utterance to echo throughout the cosmos: *"well done thy good and faithful servant"*—you are rattled by the announcement of your name summoning you to the podium. How pleasing the feel of the victor's wreath as it adorns your head (I Peter 5:4). How fascinating to make out your name etched in the record books, referred to in Revelation as *"The Lamb's Book of Life."*

None of which compare with what's next: You notice the vast sea of God's elect being parted, bringing into your view the Face of Him Whom you relentlessly chased after all these years. I do so pray for you to be locked in momentary paralysis, wondering, "which for me is far better, to keep gazing at His face or fall at His feet?"

As exhilarating as "breaking the tape" at the finish line will be that day, this race, like every race, will take preparation. Much work remains to be done. There's a race not only to be run—there's a race to be won.

It's your turn to run, to make up for lost time. If ever a time existed to receive Our Father's Word and pass it forward, that time is now. No room to fail. Second will not suffice. God is counting on us. The multitudes are, as well. So please, we bid you: Step up, step out and step onto the track. The race is about to begin. Let's get started.

Welcome to *The Relay.*

1

ADAM

The First Runner, the First Failure

"An athlete is not crowned unless he competes according to the rules."

(2 Timothy 2:5)

There is some debate about when it was discovered that Lauryn Williams was fast. Her father claims that it was when she spent an entire day at the science center in Pittsburgh racing a hologram of the legendary Olympic gold medalist Florence Joyner until she was actually able to beat it. For her mother, it was when she could beat their family dog home after playing outside. Either way, they knew that she could run—fast. — Hope Sports

AFTER being crowned NCAA Champion at the age of 20, Williams' next feat was securing her spot on the American 4x100 women's relay during the 2004 Summer Olympics.

The four women on the team were several of the fastest in the world and together, they easily had a shot at not only a gold medal, but a world record. In the end, whatever the reason, the baton failed to be passed inside of the allotted zone and the team was disqualified.

An opportunity for [Williams'] redemption presented itself at the 2008 Summer Olympics in Beijing where she qualified to run the 4x100-meter relay. The nightmare repeated itself for the American women. The baton was again dropped during the transfer; once more the team headed home empty-handed, devastated and in the merciless hands of the media. "I just wanted to hit the rewind button," says Lauryn. It seemed that one mistake was forgivable, but definitely not two. —Hope Sports

Would you have guessed that Adam, The Relay's first runner, the first failure, was also Earth's first preacher? He had the same responsibility that every preacher has — to state and administer to God's people what the God of the universe actually has to say to them. Or, as further defined by Lutheran professor David Bauslin: "Every living preacher must receive his communication direct from God, and the constant purpose of his life must be to receive it uncorrupted and to deliver it without addition or subtraction."

Take, for example, the very first command God spoke to Adam in Genesis 2:16-17: *"From any tree of the garden you may eat freely; but from the tree of the knowledge of good and evil you shall not eat, for in the day that you eat from it you will surely die."* In this instance, the Law that God entrusted to Adam, Adam in turn was to pass cleanly to Eve, "without addition or subtraction," akin to the clean baton pass in a relay like Lauryn Williams' story above. In Adam's case, this should have been a doable feat, especially in a perfect world, especially in a yet-to-be tainted Garden like the one in Eden. It was that simple. Or so one would think.

Unfortunately for him and unfortunately for us, he fumbled the baton repeatedly right out of the gate. The Relay seemed to be over before it could start. Although disqualification was certainly in order, something previously unknown took its place: grace. In a perfect world with perfect people, such a thing as grace was unnecessary. In a fallen world that man has lived in ever since, a lack of it would be unimaginable. As we will soon discover beginning in Genesis 3, God's grace is like a thick fog: It tends to settle in the lowest of places. In Adam's case, he couldn't go much lower. The Relay had to continue. Therefore, the race would go on.

During every semester that I've taught at Birmingham Theological Seminary, I've had the students read about The Fall of Man in Genesis 3:1-13. I'll preface by telling them that just as a wise jeweler knows to display his diamonds' brilliance by placing them against a dark backdrop, the Gospel's brilliance likewise shines brightest when set against a backdrop of sin and darkness. I then ask, "With all the darkness enshrouding this portion of the Old Testament, where do you see the Gospel shine brightest?" What surprises me most is not what the students find, but what they don't find. Take a minute to try and determine for yourself:

¹Now the serpent was more crafty than any beast of the field which the LORD God had made. And he said to the woman, 'Indeed, has God said, "You shall not eat from any tree of the garden"?' ²The woman said to the serpent, 'From the fruit of the trees of the garden we may eat; ³but from the fruit of the tree which is in the middle of the garden, God has said, "You shall not eat from it or touch it, or you will die."' ⁴The serpent said to the woman, 'You surely will not die! ⁵For God knows that in the day you eat from it your eyes will be opened and you will be like God, knowing good and evil.' ⁶When the woman saw that the tree was good for food and that it was a delight to the eyes and that the tree was desirable to make one wise, she took from its fruit and ate; and she gave also to her husband with her and he ate. ⁷Then the eyes of both of them were opened and they knew that they were naked; and they sewed fig leaves together and made themselves loin coverings.

"⁸They heard the sound of the LORD God walking in the garden in the cool of the day and the man and his wife hid themselves from the presence of the LORD God among the trees of the garden.

⁹Then the LORD God called to the man and said to him, 'Where are you?' ¹⁰He said, 'I heard the sound of You in the garden and I was afraid because I was naked; so I hid myself.' ¹¹And He said, 'Who told you that you were naked? Have you eaten from the tree of which I commanded you not to eat?' ¹²The man said, 'The woman whom You gave to be with me, she gave me from the tree and I ate.' ¹³Then the LORD God said to the woman, 'What is this you have done?' And the woman said, 'The serpent deceived me and I ate.'"

Many of the students' responses are good; some very good. What I'm looking for when I ask this question is, "But where's the great? Where's the brilliance?" In my experience, for a student to ever grasp just how incredibly bright the Gospel is, he must first grasp just how terribly dark sin is. For that reason, I always go through an in-depth look at Adam's dark blunders first, before we ever get to the brilliance. To that end, let's take a deeper look.

Adam's First Fumble Was Silence!

As soon as the serpent opened his mouth, he did the unthinkable: He questioned the validity of God's Word by asking, "Did God really say this?" This was the first time God's Word was challenged, and it would not be the last. Had Adam acted here, not as a passive bystander but as the man he was designed to be, the Fall might not have occurred.

Adam's Second, Third and Fourth Fumbles Were Passivity!

When asked why he was so precise in everything he did, one Puritan minister replied: "I serve a precise God." The ancient Hebrew manuscripts record precisely what God said to Adam in Genesis 2:16: *"from any tree of the garden you may eat,*

eat!" Did you notice how *"eat"* was repeated? It was repeated to add emphasis as in *"eat, eat"* of all the Garden's produce, eat all that you want, eat to your heart's desire then more. Conversely, God said that if you eat of the *"knowledge of good and evil"* tree you will surely *"die, die."* The *"die"* was repeated to express how death for Adam would be absolute: He would not only die physically, but spiritually, emotionally and relationally as well.

Now, keeping in mind precision's importance when it comes to God's Word, take a closer look at Eve's rendering of what God supposedly said:

> *"²The woman said to the serpent, 'From the fruit of the trees of the garden we may eat; ³but from the fruit of the tree which is in the middle of the garden, God has said, "You shall not eat from it or touch it, or you will die."* (Genesis 3:2-3)

Eve minimized the full force of God's Word as she used only one *"eat"* and one *"die"* rather than two. Taking away any portion of Scripture will always produce the same result: libertinism. A libertine feels life is best lived unchecked—freedom from God's law and liberty from all moral constraints. Pretty much a less-than-what-is-written interpretation of Scripture.

What's more, in verse 3, Eve randomly decided to add an extra rule of her own: *"you shall not eat from it or touch it."* God never said anything about touching the fruit. He just said don't eat it. Adding additional rules to Scripture will always produce the same result: legalism. Pretty much a more-than-what-is-written interpretation of Scripture.

Who, then, is ultimately to blame for the above falls? Adam! To speak on behalf of the God of the Universe is no small matter. He is a precise God and intends to be quoted precisely. To ensure exactness or permanence in Biblical times, let's take, for instance, the laws governing a kingdom. Each law was to be inscribed in stone by an engraver, the *chaqaq*, or lawgiver, as he was called. The *chaqaq* had no liberty to alter laws as he saw fit, and to do so was a death sentence. Because Eve didn't yet exist earlier in the narrative, Adam's commission as *chaqaq*, or lawgiver, was to relay, as in stone, God's law. He was to ensure she would be able to understand it perfectly, leaving no room for misinterpretation.

Whether he failed to relay it verbatim or failed to ensure it was clearly understood is debatable. What is not debatable is that God's Word was being grossly misrepresented by Eve as Adam stood idly by saying nothing. Adam was with her the entire time but remained deathly silent. Male passivity at its worst! The occasion when Eve extended her hand to pluck the forbidden fruit, if only Adam had extended his a little farther, gently preventing her from indulging. Instead, she ate, and then he ate, and for the first time, they found themselves out of God's Presence, hiding in the trees.

"There is a God who runs to the weary, the worn, and the weak. And the same gentle hands that hold me when I'm broken, they conquer death to bring me victory."

— "My Redeemer Lives" by Nicole Mullen

Once again, the question remains: when reading Genesis 3:1-13, "Where's the great? Where's the brilliance?" Before answering, a final hint can be found in The New Testament parable of the Prodigal Son. In short, a wayward son demanded his share of his father's inheritance even as the father was alive. The suggestion is he wished his father were dead. The son fled to a distant country where he squandered his estate with loose living.

If you are familiar with the story, do you recall where the son went when hungry? Do you recall where he went when starving? The answer is significant: When the rebellious son was hungry, he resorted to scavenging for food in a disgusting pig sty, only to look around and have to admit just how far he had fallen.

It was only then, at this breaking point of desperation, as the son faced the real possibility of starvation, that he came to his senses and turned away from the filth of the pig sty as well as his past. Getting up, he went to his Father. The Father's response? *"But while he was still a long way off, his Father saw him and felt compassion for him, and ran and embraced him and kissed him."* The sole reference to God running in the Bible is found here. The Greek word *dramo* beautifully emphasizes the point as it literally means "to spend all of one's strength in attaining something." That means our Long-Suffering God spent all His strength in attaining the wayward son where he was and as he was, away from God's Presence. And he did so long before the Prodigal Son even had the opportunity to repent.

To return briefly to Lauryn Williams' story above, shortly after her second defeat in the 2008 Olympics, insult was added to injury when she learned her father had passed away.

> Still reeling from the disappointment of the games, her pain was only worsened by not having one of her biggest encouragers on the sideline. The grief didn't fully hit her until May of the following year when, out of instinct, she picked up her phone and called her Dad. As the phone rang and rang, it finally dawned on her that he was gone, and she could never again be comforted by his counsel or encouraged by his voice.
>
> —Hope Sports

Unlike Lauryn Williams, when it came to The Fall of Man in the Garden, Adam did nothing of the sort—his first response was not to call out to the Father. Rather than longing to hear his Father's voice, he hid himself at the sound of God's Presence, lending further credence to an argument I'd like to make. A mere three words taken from Genesis 3:9 might be the single most telling phrase in all Scripture as to the kind of God we serve: *"Where are you?"*

Why would God possibly ask a question He already knew the answer to? Why would The All-Knowing God of the Universe ask a question like that? He didn't ask Adam where he was because *He* needed to know; He asked because He wanted Adam to know where He was: out of His Presence. And yet, that's precisely where God pursued him. Our God is the kind of God who pursued Adam where he was, as he was, without even a hint of repentance coming on the part of Adam. *"Where are you?"* According to author Rankin Wilbourne, "That may be the best three-word summary of the Bible in the Bible." To which I would add, the Bible is best defined as the unfolding of "God's relentless pursuit of humankind with zero intent of ever giving up."

Now, there's your great! There's your brilliance!—set clearly against the bleakest of backdrops. That chase didn't end in Eden. It's still on, even now, with you in sight.

Batons of the Invisible Sort

It always strikes me how strong an affinity Christ had for down-and-outers like the Prodigal Son—those who were marginalized, pushed to the outskirts of society. If we want to find Jesus in the four Gospels, our best chances are to look to the fringes. That's where He can most often be seen. Remember, those are the same fringes where we too were once found. Given that imitation is the greatest flattery, wouldn't you do well to imitate Christ by looking to the fringes, going there and praying in between?

Under Heaven there's a time for every season, a time to

extend a Good Word, a time to withhold it. A time to speak or to remain silent. The Bible instructs that the season is always opportune for advancing batons of the invisible sort: prayers on behalf of other people. Countless were advanced on your behalf. Invisible batons, prayers, are uniquely effective in reaching the lost, drawing our friends on the fringes back in.

> *"16Therefore, confess your sins to one another, and pray for one another so that you may be healed. The effective prayer of a righteous man can accomplish much. 17Elijah was a man with a nature like ours, and he prayed earnestly that it would not rain, and it did not rain on the earth for three years and six months. 18Then he prayed again, and the sky poured rain and the earth produced its fruit. 19My brethren, if any among you strays from the truth and one turns him back, 20let him know that he who turns a sinner from the error of his way will save his soul from death and will cover a multitude of sins." (James 5:16-20)*

If bad news travels fast, then news of a pastor's errant daughter in a small town travels faster. As the pastor was getting up to teach the midweek service, several ladies of the church requested that he postpone his lesson in lieu of a prayer service for his daughter. The entire congregation, as well as the entire town, had heard how fast and hard the daughter had been running; she'd been running many months at the time, as hard as any could possibly run, but in the wrong direction, away from her faith. The pastor agreed to oblige this once; however, at the ladies' insistence, the prayer would continue over the course of the next six weeks. One evening, as the man stood in his kitchen, his daughter whom he'd not seen in months burst through the back door falling to her knees, clinging to his legs. Crying out through the sobs, she pleaded, "Tell them to stop, tell them they must stop, tell them they have to stop." Knowing that the rough kids she'd been running with had obviously wronged his daughter, anger began welling up inside. "Whoever it is who is praying for me, please tell them to stop. I'm begging you Daddy, please tell them to stop. I can't take it anymore. Tell them to stop praying."

As God pursued Adam in the Garden, so did these women of the church pursue the pastor's daughter, and so are you to pursue those around you. Starting today, as you run, imitate Christ by looking to the fringes, going there, and praying in between. Notch up your prayer life beginning tomorrow morning. Start early. Commit to a solid 20 minutes of prayer on behalf of the lost before you leave home. Very likely, the recipient will remain unaware of the prayers you offer. Very likely, you will remain unaware of the result. For certain, the Lord commands it. Trust He will use it as He may.

Ours is the God of Second Chances

What the first Adam made wrong, the second Adam (Christ) made right. Because of Jesus our race continues, albeit in a fallen world. Ours is a life lived between two gardens—one fallen, the other redeemed; bodies bruised, even scarred (indeed, even the resurrected Jesus kept His scars); batons routinely dropped.

Success, according to William Faulkner, "seems to be largely a matter of hanging on after others have let go." More and more I find myself drawn to the *"more than conquerors"* (Romans 8:37), competitors like you who are *"afflicted in every way, but not crushed; perplexed, but not despairing; persecuted, but not forsaken; struck down, but not destroyed."* (2nd Corinthians 4:8–9)

This reminds me time and again that *"momentary, light affliction is producing for us an eternal weight of glory far beyond all comparison."* (2nd Corinthians 4:17) Tragedy historically produces Christianity's greatest triumphs. Personally, I've found it is far easier to love an overcomer's story than to live one.

They inject me with hope, keep me on the track when prone to stray, force me to retrieve downed batons and hang on after others have let go.

What about you? Surely you have a story of overcoming to share, or perhaps you're trudging through one even now. I need to hear your story, your coworkers need to hear it, random acquaintances need to hear it as well. It's called a personal testimony, and only you can tell it. It's what a relay runner passing the baton looks like.

Write your testimony down on paper, include at least two Bible verses that impacted you, carry it in your pocket if you have to and rehearse it until you get it down to two minutes. That way you'll be able to share it on the spur of the moment. Next, ask God to provide you with a Divine Appointment to tell it. When the appointment arrives, start speaking before your mind talks you out of it.

Or for those of you who are presently running strong and yet to be wearied, be advised that the comfort of Isaiah 40:29-31 will only go so far. For the rest of us familiar with life's foes, we can testify to having seen its words morph into life: *"He gives strength to the weary, And to him who lacks might He increases power. Though youths grow weary and tired, And vigorous young men stumble badly, Yet those who wait for the LORD Will gain new strength; They will mount up with wings like eagles, They will run and not get tired, They will walk and not become weary."*

Regardless of where you are in your momentary afflictions, on behalf of a centuries-old chain of faithful Christians, listen to our appeal: Please do not abandon the race before finishing. After all, it's not just your race, it's ours!

It's Not Just Your Race, It's Ours

Pastor John MacArthur shared the following story from his college years:

I was running in the 4x400-meter relay at the Orange
County Invitational. As a baseball player moonlighting in
track and field, I wasn't the fastest runner on our team.
So, I ran the second leg.

Our strategy was simple. The first runner, a speedy
sprinter, would get as big a lead as possible right out of
the starting blocks. My job was merely to run a clean lap
without dropping the baton. Our third man was strong
and fast, and our fourth man was a blur. They could
make up whatever ground I might lose.

Our first man ran a great leg and made a perfect baton pass. I managed to finish my lap in a tight battle for
first place. The third man went around the curve, came
halfway down the backstretch, stopped, walked off, and
sat down in the grass. The race kept going.

We thought he had pulled a hamstring or twisted an
ankle. We all ran across the infield, expecting to find him
writhing on the grass or at least wincing in pain. He wasn't.
He was sitting passively. We anxiously asked, "What happened? Are you hurt?" He said, "No, I'm OK. I just didn't
feel like running."

MacArthur went on to conclude:

My teammates and I spontaneously responded with an
outpouring of frustration, all three of us basically saying
the same thing: "You can't do that! You're not in this by
yourself! Do you realize the effort we have all put into
training for this? Too much has been invested in you!"
Anyone who breaks that centuries-old chain is like a relay runner who abandons the race before finishing. And
what's at stake in this race is infinitely more important
than any earthly trophy. Failure to run well and with endurance would be an inexcusable insult to our Lord, an

Regardless of where you are in your momentary afflictions, on behalf of a centuries-old chain of faithful Christians listen to your appeal: Please do not abandon the race before finishing. After all, it's not just your race, it's ours!

offense against those who have taught us, a disappointment to those who have trained alongside us, and a grievous sin against those to whom we must hand the baton.

In closing, I'd like to share an "Administration of the Word" story of my own that might spur you to act:

Slipping off to do nothing more than think, I found my way into the back of Grace Chapel in the fall of 1996. Orientation was taking place for the incoming freshmen at Reformed Theological Seminary in Jackson, Mississippi. Looking back, the most significant transitional experience of my ministry occurred within my going in and my going out that day. No more than 15 minutes between the two. It was a subtle, albeit significant, threshold, nonetheless.

It was the chapel's utter simplicity that confused me most: devoid of any stained-glass windows, kneelers, crosses, a baptismal, all the things one would normally expect to see inside. What I did see no eye could ever miss: a raised pulpit, very raised in fact, 10 feet in the air; and a stairwell stood beneath. Easing up just shy of the stairwell's base, to go any further would seem irreverent until the right moment had come, I tried to make sense of why the sanctuary had been constructed in such a peculiar way. I was impressed with the subtle recognition that the blueprints were no accident. Far from it.

Grace Chapel's lack of adornment by design conveyed an essential message—that the highest ideal on campus was to elevate the primacy of the Word of God above all else, in all that we do. Had the decades of graduates been able to speak in one collective voice there in that space, I'd bet they would say: "If you get nothing else from your time here, you must get this . . . you must get Jesus. You must get His Word."

It would be another two and a half long years before I stood again at the base of that stairwell. My chance to preach had finally come. Ascending those steps for the first time, settling behind the grand pulpit, looking down from the perched loft, even after all these years, the sole word I can think to describe what I sensed in that moment was "rightness." "Rightness" has since become one of my favorite words. My "rightness" immediately morphed into a "weightiness" the second a small five-word placard caught my eye: **"Sir, we would see Jesus."**

Never before then and rarely since, have I been so overcome as to be unable to preach. I do so hope that never changes. Should the day arrive when I feel no weightiness at **"Sir, we would see Jesus,"** I wish that anyone reading this might so care for the Gospel's integrity that compulsion would have you say, "brother, it's time you change fields." I also pray that I be given the wherewithal to receive any such admonition.

Two questions to pose in closing this chapter:

First, what if—and I intend this more as a suggestion than a question—what if you religiously sought the Lord's favor, asking Him to please embed within you, to chase Christ in such desperate manner that a placard in summary of your life might one day read, "We didn't see _____, we saw Jesus."

Second, if a placard were to be written in summary of your life today, how might it read? (Check all that apply.)

- ☐ Modest progress, but at least she didn't drop the baton
- ☐ "You who were running so well; who hindered you from obeying the truth?" (Galatians 5:7)
- ☐ His string of second chances finally ran out
- ☐ A life lived in relentless pursuit of Christ
- ☐ I saw him in church, but never recall hearing him talk openly about spiritual matters
- ☐ Her faith is being proclaimed throughout the whole world!" (Romans 1:8)
- ☐ She fell down but got back up

Whatever your answer, take this to heart: As long as you are alive, nothing has been unalterably etched in stone. Which means that you, unlike an ancient lawgiver such as Adam, mercifully have time to make changes and engrave a life story of your own. Be optimistic and leave a lot of space to be filled with names of those you will bring into the race. No one will automatically join. People may see Jesus in you, but they need to hear the unique changes He has brought about in your life. Become that relay runner who invests in others as others invested in you by telling at least one person your testimony tomorrow. Please do it; we need you.

2

MOSES

Indeed, It Is Your Life!

"These words, which I am commanding you today, shall be on your heart.
"You shall teach them diligently to your sons and shall talk of them when
you sit in your house and when you walk by the way and when you lie down
and when you rise up." (Deuteronomy 6:6-7)

When I was 18, a friend owned a condominium in the Cayman Islands, and he allowed my family to stay there for a week. The first day we arrived, we immediately set out to find a special spot to snorkel. The coral reef we found was nothing short of spectacular. Floating over its surface, I could see the bottom of the ocean floor, guessing it to be about five feet away. Diving down a little way to touch the reef should have been an achievable feat. Interestingly enough, after descending at least 10 or so feet, I was unable to touch the bottom. Swimming back to the surface, I began reasoning to myself that the plane flight must have altered my depth perception. I knew what I saw. That reef was only a few feet away—it was right there! Taking a much deeper breath, I swam down farther, around 15 feet deep, and still came up short. Exasperated, I did not understand what just happened. Finally, I overheard our guide sharing how the coral reef was 30 feet beneath the ocean's surface. I realized that although I could see the bottom as clear as crystal, no matter how hard I tried I could never reach it.

In the same manner, Saint Augustine, an early church leader, summarized Scripture's vastness this way: "Though I see the depths, I can never reach the bottom." To pierce the Bible's deepest depth is an impossibility. I would contend, however, that it would be inexcusable for us not to try.

Never was I more acutely aware of this reality than my first day of class at Reformed Theological Seminary in 1996. I was like a sponge ready to soak up every ounce of truth this institution of higher learning had to offer.

With no particular fanfare, Old Testament Professor Dr. Currid entered the classroom. I found it particularly strange how unusually solemn the atmosphere was; first-day jitters, I supposed. Dr. Currid's lecture opened with Deuteronomy 32:46-47, which he proceeded to read: *"Take to your heart all the words with which I am warning you today, which you shall command your sons to observe carefully, even all the words of this law. For it is not an idle word for you; indeed, it is your life! And by this word you will prolong your days in the land, which you are about to cross the Jordan to possess."*

After listening to those obscure verses, I thought to myself, "what a peculiar place to begin for our first lecture." Three hours later, I concluded, "what a brilliant place to have begun!" More like scuba divers than snorkelers, we breached inner layer upon inner layer of undiscovered depths beneath the vast expanse of God's Holy Script without once coming up for air. Upon dismissal after his three-hour lecture, Dr. Currid had only taught two out of the Old Testament's 23,145 verses. I give my word: the bottom was nowhere in sight. Not even close.

If we were to go back in Biblical history and enter the original setting of Deuteronomy 32, we would quickly note how Moses had the complete and undivided attention of his people for his departing sermon. After all, what else could his captive audience of Jewish brothers and sisters do but idly sit and wait in the desert as they'd done for the last 40 years? The encamped settlers on the Jordan River's eastern bank, along the Plains of Moab, were happy to lend their ears to their leader, at least for now. All sensed that something big was at hand; a new beginning, in fact, was just beyond the River and Moses had them transfixed. At the ripe old age of 120, he had amassed treasure troves of otherworldly wisdom that he was eager to impart to his people. With but two months remaining on his life's lease to make his final pleas, the fiery pitch of his messages became increasingly fevered.

To underscore the profound impact Moses' farewell sermon had on his listeners, consider these four truths:

1. **It was a "do-over" sermon** directed toward second-time listeners. He'd preached it previously. They'd already heard it, and they'd hear it again. In his introduction, *"the words with which I am warning you today,"* the Hebrew word for "warning" means "to repeat" or "do over." Repetition in the Bible is replete with deeper meaning—it's God's way of grabbing us by the shoulders and exclaiming, "Do not miss this!!"

2. **It was a song or an anthem** *"which was the duty and care of magistrates to make well known by frequent repetition."* (Jamieson, Fausset and Brown) How better to memorize wise sayings than putting them to music?

3. **It was a monumental juncture in the passing of the baton.** Moses concluded with next steps: *"and by this word you will prolong your days in the land, which you are about to cross the Jordan to possess"* (32:47). *Abar* in Hebrew means "from hand to hand," or in English "to cross." Identical to a baton passing from hand to hand in a relay, the words Moses handed off to the Israelites were in turn

to be handed off to their children, who in turn were to hand off to succeeding generations . . . "hand to hand to hand to hand" as the Jews "crossed" *(abar) the Jordan."*

4. **It quite possibly contains the weightiest string of five words in the entirety of Scripture** and it served as the key verse behind the impetus for this book: *"Indeed, it is your life!"* In contrast to the first five words uttered by the serpent in Genesis 3, which undermined the validity of what God said (*"Indeed, has God really said?"*), Moses affirmed the Lord's utterances, elevating them to the highest of pedestals. In essence, he was stating, "If I could only hand off one baton to you . . . just one baton that not only contains the 'words of life' but in every sense 'is your life' it would be the Word of God." The Scriptures God breathed out for His people are by design like a garment: Though differing threads are used to make it, they are interwoven in such a fashion that it becomes impossible to extract one from the other. So it is with the believer and the Law.

If by chance you're still unconvinced about how major the implications are from his message, two questions for you to contemplate:

First, "If your home were burning down and you could run in to save only one most prized possession, what would it be?" Isn't it fascinating how quickly one's collection of stuff can so instantly diminish in value? Let's call that one prized possession **perspective.** Moses's perspective was not clouded by stuff: He never owned much of anything; very possibly nothing. But from his way of seeing things, had his Holy Land Excursion gone up in flames, he would not have had a moment's hesitation about which prized possession to retrieve and pass forward: the Book of the Law, The Torah.

Second, Moses wrote more of the Bible than any single author: 79,976 words to be exact. If those 79,976 words could be encapsulated in a single sentence, wouldn't it only make sense for someone to give that sentence the strongest consideration? Yes and yes!

You see, as Moses exclaimed, *"indeed, it is your life!"* he realized he possessed eternity's sole treasure guaranteed to outlive Earth and outlast Heaven: *"Heaven and earth will pass away, but My words will not pass away."* (Mark 13:31) It was a treasure he was forbidden to hoard and commanded to pass forward—*"the very words of God."* His demand is that you obtain it, not **as if** your life depends on it but **because** your life depends on it. To put it matter-of-factly: Your obtainment of Christ and His words must reach the state where it becomes impossible to extricate one from the other.

One of the greatest preachers of all time, Charles Spurgeon, described this state of being well by saying, "Oh, that you and I might get into the very heart of the Word of God, and get that Word into ourselves! As I have seen the silkworm eat into the leaf, and consume it, so ought we to do with the Word of the Lord—not crawl over its surface, but eat right into it till we have taken it into our inmost parts."

He then referenced John Bunyan, the author of *Pilgrim's Progress,* as one such example: "Why, this man is a living Bible! Prick him anywhere; his blood is Bibline, the very essence of the Bible flows from him. He cannot speak without quoting a text, for his very soul is full of the Word of God!"

Directly antithetical to bleeding Bibline, is a deadly epidemic rapidly spreading across the globe called Gospel Inoculation. This condition occurs when the tiniest amount of Gospel is introduced in a person's life—enough to make him feel safe but effectively immune from being totally overtaken by Christ and His word. Much like being vaccinated. Telltale warning signs include apathy, Gospel Fatigue and a

It'd be intriguing to stop here and ask, if a continuum were drawn with **Consumed by the Gospel** at one end and **Apathetic to the Gospel** at the other, where would those who know you best mark the X where you'd be found?

⟵————————————⟶

Consumed by the Gospel   **Apathetic to the Gospel**

If the X that marks the spot is farther right than you prefer, you have the power to change it. Change does not occur on its own; it takes discipline, the same root word as disciple. Discipline yourself to spend a set amount of time reading your Bible each morning. Set a timer if you need to. The return on time invested will pay dividends. Gospel in, Gospel out.

false sense of wellness: *"I have no need of a physician!"* (Matthew 9:12) The pathology report reads, "Ineffective as a runner. Ineligible to run The Relay."

This World Is Not My Home

One might say: "This is all fine and good, but where does Christ fit into this equation? In the New Testament, Paul said, *'for to me to live is Christ.'* So, which is it? Is my life 'the Word' that Moses spoke of? Or is my life 'Christ' as Paul said?"

The answer is simple—both, in the person of Jesus. He and His Word are one and the same. To have complete union with Christ is to have complete union with His Word and vice-versa.

Look how John's Gospel opens with an emphatic declaration: *"In the beginning was the Word, the Word was with God, and the Word was God."* (John 1:1) Jesus further clarified, *"if you believed Moses, you would believe Me, for he wrote about Me. But if you do not believe his writings, how will you believe My words?"* (John 5:46-47)

All throughout the New Testament, Jesus would constantly point His listeners to the Scriptures which, in turn, pointed back to Him. *"And beginning with Moses and all the Prophets, He explained to them what was said in all the Scriptures concerning Himself."* (Luke 24:27) Or what about Philip, the soon-to-be disciple who drew a similar conclusion? *"We have found Him of whom Moses in the Law and also the Prophets wrote—Jesus of Nazareth, the son of Joseph . . . come and see!"* (John 1:45-46)

Frankly, the better question is: If your life is Christ and Christ is the Word, are you communing with Him by frequenting His Teachings? Or, are you neglecting the very thing that Moses said is, in fact, your life?

Let me be very clear: To neglect time in the Word is to neglect time with Jesus. You cannot have One without the other.

"If you abide in Me, and My words abide in you, ask whatever you wish, and it will be done for you. My Father is glorified by this, that you bear much fruit, and so prove to be My disciples." (John 15:7-8)

Disciples of Jesus are to be "foot-travelers" while on Earth, never staying put for long. It's like country music legend "Gentleman Jim" Reeves' country hit that says, "This world is not my home, I'm just a-passin' through."

I cannot emphasize enough: Abiding with your Redeemer daily as a discipline is so critical because it allows God to strengthen you and sustain you as you run through this life. It's really no different than what sustained the Jews while they wandered in the desert wilderness: daily manna.

> "Are you burning with fever? He is the Spring to refresh you. Are you bound down by your sins? He is the Liberator. Are you in need of help? He is Strength. Are you afraid of death? He is Life. Are you longing for Heaven? He is the way. Are you fleeing from darkness? He is Light. Are you in need of sustenance? He is Bread."
>
> —Saint Ambrose

Not as Good as it Gets . . . Not Even Close

I simply cannot fathom being stranded in the center of a Middle Eastern desert for any length of time; not for days, not for weeks, not for months, certainly not for years. The sand, the heat, the monotonous landscape, the boredom—and more sand. To have any shot at survival, I would have to affix my eyes on the hope that there must be something far greater still just beyond. Of necessity, I would force myself to envision daily a given destination, one that was real, touchable . . . just beyond the horizon to strive for . . . to survive for. Such as a plush land of great hope and promise. Knowing it was there, very real although very unseen, might just be enough to sustain me and keep me pressing forward. Like the proverbial horse ever in pursuit of a dangling carrot just beyond reach, a chance exists, albeit a very small one, of perhaps reaching it one day.

Even if I had limitless hope, hope in and of itself would not see me through. There would have to be more, much more. Wholly dependent on God, He would have to provide my daily sustenance, basic physical necessities like bread and water. Never letting the suspicion escape my notice: "I sense He takes great joy in leaving the impression He's one step ahead of my every 'give us this day our daily bread' prayer." Such a Wise Master to allot an exacted portion for me—not too much, not too little, but just what is right. He knows full well that excess sustenance before me **right here** would detour my affections away from **out there**. He's good that way.

That exact scenario can be the only plausible explanation for what carried the Jews through their desert wandering some 3,500 years ago. Immediately after the Israelites broke free from the yoke of their Egyptian oppressors, they ventured into a real and seemingly endless Middle Eastern Desert. Early in the journey, they held their heads high, confident that as the chosen people of The Almighty, the good hand of their Lord was upon them. After all, it was He who promised, *"I will bring you to the land which I swore to give to Abraham, Isaac, and Jacob, and I will give it to you for a possession; I am the Lord.'"* (Exodus 6:8)

Little did they know then, what should have been an eight-day journey would drag on for 40 laborious years. Humans, like hope, are dependent upon a fuel source to survive. Facing an endless sea of sand surrounding every side, they found no such fuel. Both humans and their hope started dying on the vine.

"But God"—two of the most fitting words for God's impeccable timeliness—the Self-proclaimed One rich in mercy and abounding in loving kindness rained down grace upon grace from Heaven in the form of manna, a wafer-like substance, at every sunrise. Moses described it as *"a fine flake-like thing, fine as the frost on the ground."* (Exodus 16:14)

There was, however, one major stipulation in the form of a daily test graded upon faith. The lesson learned was one of unmitigated dependence: God alone will provide. *"Then the LORD said to Moses, "Behold, I will rain bread from Heaven for you; and the people shall go out and gather a day's portion every day, that I may test them, whether or not they will walk in My instruction."* (Exodus 16:4)

Yahweh only allowed the sojourners to gather enough provision to get them through each day, one day at a time; nothing more, nothing less. Recalling the landscape, can you imagine the ever-present temptation to not store up for a dry and arid day? The lesson was not an act **of** faith but an act **on** faith—"as He provided for me today, I'm trusting Him to provide for me tomorrow."

"Faith is the assurance of things hoped for, the conviction of things not seen. For by it the men of old gained approval. By faith we understand that the worlds were prepared by the word of God." (Hebrews 11:2-3)

The grave danger for our modern lives is this (which also accounts for a surprisingly weak modern faith): With an ever-increasing appetite to accumulate that which can be seen, little appetite remains for the *"conviction of things not seen."*

Stated differently, our insatiable want chokes out our basic need. It seems we've made our own version of manna in the form of consumerism, commercialism and materialism. We've deceived ourselves into believing our supply is unlimited. Therefore faith, trust and hope appear to be unnecessary, or maybe even archaic. If we're not careful, we might find ourselves stuck somewhere we don't belong.

Take the following analogy, for instance. Imagine that the Israelites, while wandering, happened upon an oasis, a gigantic storehouse full of the latest and greatest this world has to offer. Before long, they might have become so attached, viewing themselves as completely self-reliant, and decided to take up permanent residence there . . . in a desert, no less!

Growing quite chummy and chubby, biding their own sweet time, God's promise of a Land flowing with milk and honey would lose all allure. Oblivious to the fact that their storehouses will at some point empty, the following parable speaks to their folly:

> *"The land of a rich man was very productive. And he began reasoning to himself, saying, 'What shall I do, since I have no place to store my crops?' Then he said, 'This is what I will do: I will tear down my barns and build larger ones, and there I will store all my grain and my goods. And I will say to my soul, "Soul, you have many goods laid up for many years to come; take your ease, eat, drink and be merry."' But God said to him, 'You fool! This very night your soul is required of you; and now who will own what you have prepared?' So is the man who stores up treasure for himself and is not rich toward God."*
> (Luke 12:16-21)

A lot of good exists in the world. I, for one, enjoy being here. But for the Christian, this is not as good as it gets, not even close. So, the challenge for you is this: If your goal is to win Heaven, you'll get Earth thrown in. If your goal is to win Earth, you'll get neither.

For the sake of fellow runners in the field and to all who will soon join, please aim to win Heaven; your undertaking is paramount to our success.

Moses by the Numbers

If ever Scripture presented a runner whose life exemplified a relay, it would have to be Moses. His race of faith could be evenly divided into four legs: three of which he'd run on his own, but sadly he could only go so far.

If your goal is to win Heaven, you'll get Earth thrown in. If your goal is to win Earth, you'll get neither.

Due to a prior transgression against The Lord his Provider, a "No Trespassing" sign erected on the Jordan's easternmost edge blocked any further progress. Sin and its consequences do take their toll. For that fourth and final leg, he would have to hand the controls to another: *"Joshua is the one who will cross ahead of you, just as the Lord has spoken."* (Deuteronomy 31:3)

- Moses' first leg — running Egypt for 40 years

- Moses' second leg — outrunning God for 40 years

- Moses' third leg — running to and through the powers that be for 40 years

- The fourth and final leg — Joshua is the anchor who succeeded him

A most extraordinary occasion in the life of Moses, moreover the life of Israel, took place while he encountered his God on an obscure mountain named Horeb. It would set the stage for a sequence of cataclysmic events, the likes of which this world had never before seen—the 10 plagues in Egypt. It would help explain Moses' lifelong repeated, urgent, even obsessive appeals: *"You must get this . . . you must get His Word!"*

The scene played out like this: As an 80-year-old, Moses was a shepherd tending sheep in a foreign land when Yahweh appeared to him from a burning bush: *"Therefore, come now, and I will send you to Pharaoh, so that you may bring My people, the sons of Israel, out of Egypt."* (Exodus 3:10)

Crippled by fear, he began offering pitiful excuses:

♦ "I'm a nobody." (*"Who am I that I should go to Pharaoh?"* Exodus 3:11)

♦ "I don't even know Your Name." (*"They may say to me, 'What is His name?' What shall I say to them?'"* Exodus 3:13)

♦ "Nobody will listen to me." (*"What if they will not believe me or listen to what I say?"* Exodus 4:1)

♦ "I am a pathetic communicator." (*"I have never been eloquent, neither recently nor in time past, nor since You have spoken to Your servant; for I am slow of speech and slow of tongue."* Exodus 4:10)

♦ "How about sending someone else?" (*"Please, Lord, now send the message by whomever You will."* Exodus 4:13)

Needless to say, Moses' comfort zone had shrunk to the few square feet of dirt beneath him. As one adage puts it: "Your world will expand for every step you dare to take outside your comfort zone."

You too have a comfort zone defined by similar self-imposed constraints. It will not expand an inch if you allow that naysaying self-talk voice to sabotage your mind. Do these sound familiar?

☐ "I'm awkward talking about Christianity. I get nervous. I don't know what I'm supposed to say. It's not like I have a seminary degree." (Just like when Moses said, *"Who am I that I should go to Pharaoh?"*)

☐ "I don't know the Bible like I should. I mix up the stories and verses. I can't find all the answers to the questions." (Akin to what Moses said, "They may say to me, 'What is His name?' What shall I say to them?'")

☐ "My Bible study leader is better with evangelism than I
am. My friend knows the Bible backwards and for-
wards. I don't." (Comparable to Moses who asked,
"How about sending someone else?")

The excuses Moses offered may slightly differ from your own,
but the result is the same: You tell yourself, "I'm not up to
the task." Nothing could be further from the truth.

As an exercise, the second this mistruth pops up in your
head and talks you out of being bold, refute it immediately
with a Biblical truth. That will allow you to replace the naysaying before it gets a chance to take root. For example, you
can cut short the, "I don't know what I'm supposed to . . . "
thought before it's finished and replace it with, *"the Holy Spirit
will teach me what I'm supposed to say."* (Luke 12:12)

Put yourself in Moses' sandals. And remember, if someone
like Moses could undergo such a radical transformation—
note how quickly his reluctance and hesitation morphed into
unbridled boldness—the same change can occur in you.

When Moses offered his excuses, how did God respond?
He asked, *"What's in your hand?"* Any time God asks a question He already knows the answer to, start digging for deeper
meaning. In this case, the deeper meaning can be seen in
Moses' ego-deflating reply: "Just this stick."

Unlike the royal scepter he previously extended to his
humble servants in Egypt, now all he had in hand was a
lousy stick. Even if all he had was a staff, at least that would
have signified he owned the flocks he was tending. As it
stood, he didn't.

I believe it was at this point that Moses came to a place
of considerable discovery along the following lines: If a mere
stick, as an extension of The Almighty's hand, can become
the mightiest staff able to devour snakes, divide great seas

and overthrow Earth's powers that be . . . How far greater must the *sword of the Spirit* be at every believer's disposal, which is the Word of God? (Ephesians 6:17)

Because up until this point in Exodus, not once do we find a single historical record of Moses invoking God's Name or quoting God's Word during the first 80 years of his life. Not once. After a long wait, in Exodus 5:1 we finally see Moses brandish that greatest weapon of all by quoting the word, *"Thus sayeth Yahweh."*

From that point forward, Moses' "sword" would never again return to its sheath. Which is not surprising considering *"the Word of God is living and active and sharper than any two-edged sword and piercing as far as the division of soul and spirit, of both joints and marrow, and able to judge the thoughts and intentions of the heart."* (Hebrews 4:12)

Ten plagues later, Pharaoh and his demoralized Egyptian Empire were forced to relent, saying: *"Rise up, get out from among my people, both you and the sons of Israel; and go, worship the LORD, as you have said."* With *"belts fastened, sandals on feet, staffs in hand"* the Israelites prepared to make haste and congregated behind their fearless leader, his sword in hand. (Exodus 12)

Thus explains the backdrop of where this chapter initially began: At the ripe old age of 120, Moses had amassed treasure troves of otherworldly wisdom that he was eager to impart to his people. With but two months remaining on his life's lease to make his final pleas, the fiery pitch of his messages became increasingly fevered.

Then Moses said to them, *"Take to your heart all the words with which I am warning you today, which you shall command your sons to observe carefully, even all the words of this law. For it is not an idle word for you; Indeed, it is your life!"* (Deuteronomy 32)

The 40 years were up, the day of departure had arrived. That is for everyone except Moses. Shortly to be gathered to his people, even Abraham, Isaac and Jacob, his lifelong race would draw to its conclusion on the peaks of Mount Nebo; by himself, isolated and alone. Atop that mountain, his aged eyes could peer far over and deep into that Land of Promise his people yearned to behold 430 years prior. Unable to touch, much less to taste, the flowing milk and wild honey within, armed with only manna and water, I'd bet he was happy to make do. After all, he knew what was coming next.

The torch passed to Joshua, his wait in the wings now over. His appointment? To pick up exactly where Moses left off, spearheading the charge of one of history's most monumental events: the crossing of the River Jordan. At long last, The Lord's chosen people, Israel, were finally coming home.

3

JOSHUA

This Book Shall Not Depart From Your Mouth

"Great things may come to those who wait. But only the things left by those who hustle." —*Abraham Lincoln*

"As any track coach will testify, relay races are won or lost in the transfer of the baton. There's a critical moment when all may be lost by a fumble or a miscalculation. The baton is rarely dropped on the back side of the track when the runner has it firmly in his grasp. If failure is to occur, it will likely happen in the exchange between generations."

— Dr. James Dobson

Having been trained under the tutelage of his mentor for years, Joshua had no problem picking up where Moses left off. A cleaner exchange of the baton between generations cannot be found in Scripture. If you compare Moses's final goodbye east of the Jordan River: *"by **this word** you will prolong your days in the land, which you are about to cross the Jordan to possess, (Deuteronomy 32:47)* with Joshua's introductory charge west of the Jordan River: *"remember **the word** which Moses the servant of the LORD commanded you, saying 'The Lord your God gives you rest and will give you this land,'"* (Joshua 1:13) the transfer is unmistakable.

The futuristic movie *Gattaca* took sibling rivalry to a whole new level. Vincent and Anton were brothers, but Vincent was the weaker of the two and genetically inferior to Anton. Since Anton's genes were perfect, he always had the upper hand. A favorite competition of theirs was to swim out from shore and keep swimming, no matter how far, until one chickened out. The first one to turn back for shore would lose. Anton always won.

That all changed during one particular challenge; this time things were different as Vincent describes:

> "It was the last time we swam together and out into the open sea. Like always, we knew each stroke to the horizon was one we'd have to make back to the shore. But something was very different about that day. Every time Anton tried to pull away, he found me right beside him. Until finally, the impossible happened. It was the one moment in our lives that my brother was not as strong as he believed, and I was not as weak. It was the moment that made everything else possible."

Shocked by the unexpected loss, Anton inquired, "How did you do it?" To which Vincent replied: "You want to know how I did it Anton? I'll tell you how I did it! I never saved anything for the swim back!"

When studying the life of Joshua in the book that bears his name, we could say that he, too, never saved anything for the swim back. Once his countrymen passed through the River Jordan, they passed a point of no return. Turning back was not an option—not for anyone.

Joshua, designated by God as "a man who has the Spirit in him," (Numbers 27:18) was uniquely gifted as a military commander. Under his leadership over a seven-year span, the Israelites won an unprecedented string of conquests over the

Promised Land's previous inhabitants: the Canaanites. The battles were so lopsided historians are left baffled. Yet three key factors led to his unsurpassed accomplishments: First, Moses helped propel Joshua's ministry forward. Second, "all of God's promises are "yes" and "amen." Third, Joshua took the first step. We will look at each in greater detail below.

Moses as a Starting Block

Starting blocks were first used in Olympic competition at the 1948 London Games. Blocks help runners quickly accelerate by giving them something to push off from at the beginning of a race, much like a launching pad. Moses served as a type of starting block from which Joshua could launch forward.

For example, when the Law was given to Moses on Mount Sinai, only Joshua was present. When Moses entered the Tabernacle to speak directly with God, only Joshua stood guard. For that *"Indeed, it is your life"* sermon, Joshua was standing right by Moses' side. When the time came for Joshua to branch out on his own, Moses had built up for him a lifetime of solid teachings as a secure footing from which he could quickly accelerate.

All of God's Promises Are "Yes and Amen" (II Corinthians 1:20)

With absolute certainty, Joshua knew weeks in advance before the battle's first blood was shed who would end up victorious. His assurance didn't stem from self-confidence, though the Lord commanded three times that he be "bold and courageous." (Joshua 1:6–9) Neither did his assurance stem from confidence in what the Lord might do. Faith played no part. Look closely at what God told him in Joshua 1:1–3:

"Now it came about after the death of Moses the servant of the LORD, that the LORD spoke to Joshua the son of Nun, Moses' servant, saying, 'Moses My servant is dead; now therefore arise, cross this Jordan, you and all this people, to the land which I am giving to them, to the sons of Israel. Every place on which the sole of your foot treads, I have given it to you, just as I spoke to Moses.'"

Does anything perplexing stand out with the tense God used here? As in describing a future event that had not yet taken place? You see, the Lord's promises are so guaranteed to be kept (all God's promises are "yes and amen"), that He can speak of their future completion as if they'd already happened . . . in the past tense! "I have given you this land!" Though it has not yet been done, I have done it already. Before the first sole of a Hebrew's foot trod on enemy soil, the land was already theirs for the taking. War's atrocities would not be spared, such as defeat at Ai, but *"the victory already belonged to the Lord."*

Personally, that truth has ministered to me for a long time when warring through atrocities of my own, with depression, above all; it gave me some semblance of comfort knowing "the ultimate victory belongs to my Lord."

Joshua Took the First Step

Prior to 1988, the Nike Corporation faced a formidable challenge:

> The Nike brand was only speaking to a narrow range of male athletes in competitive sports arenas. There was a need to become relevant to wider circles of people, including women and baby boomer fitness enthusiasts. The actual role that fitness plays in people's lives, the actual

experience of really working out, doing aerobics, going on a bike ride, etc. has the effect of lifting people's moods and spirit. But none of this was captured in the way that Nike was communicating up to that point.

—Jerome Conlon, "The Brand Brief Behind Nike's Just Do It Campaign," *Branding Strategy Insider*

Cofounder Bill Bowerman observed that "everyone has a body and is therefore a potential athlete."

The only solution, according to one executive, was a marriage between the athlete and the rest of us:

Daily participation in sports and fitness gives people something very profound, which is an experience and feeling of joy, a runner's high, a lightness of being. This inner glow of the sports experience is the secret center to the sport categories 'experiential appeal.' This inner-joy experience was real, and all that Nike had to do in its communications was figure out a way to tap into this spirit and become a protagonist for all that was good and true about it. This was emphasized. Nike, at this point in time, had an opportunity to become the protagonist of all that was great and uplifting about the experience of sports and fitness.

—Jerome Conlon

The result was Nike's "Just Do It" ad campaign that first aired in 1988. The 30-second commercial opens by zooming in on 80-year-old runner Walt Stack as he crosses the Golden Great Bridge, part of his daily 17-mile routine. Apart from Stack's humorous line, "people ask me how I keep my teeth from chattering in the wintertime . . . 'I leave 'em in my locker,'" there's little fanfare.

In less than a decade, Nike's share of the athletic shoe market skyrocketed from 8% to 43%, and from $877 million in sales to $9.2 billion. "Just Do It" became the most iconic company slogan of all time. What accounted for its meteoric success? Its sheer simplicity: Don't just stand there ... do something. Whatever it is, just do it!

When it came to Joshua and God's call on his life, by no means did he misinterpret God's message, *"I have given you this land,"* as license to head for the sidelines and just do nothing. Not at all.

The distinction between what **God** does and what **we** do is significant, especially as it relates to the main theme of this book: Handing off our faith.

God rarely unfolds His plan on Earth wholly independent from human participation. He certainly can, but rarely does. For example, how did the conquest of the Holy Land occur? Human participation. How will His Message spread to the globe's four corners? Human participation.

This distinction was emphasized by the New Testament author James, who explained how God implants His Word in us so that it *"is able to save your souls."* (James 1:24) That is an amazing truth even when standing on its own. However, James did not stop there, but further admonished his readers: *"prove yourselves doers of the Word, and not merely hearers who delude themselves! One who looks intently at the perfect law, the law of liberty, and abides by it, not having become a forgetful hearer but an effectual doer, this man will be blessed in what he does."* (James 1:22, 25)

Read the scenario below and try to imagine how you might have handled it.

Prior to leaving for a week's vacation, a junior high track coach gathered together the team's standouts, expressing the need for others to pick up the slack in her absence— maintaining cohesion, guarding against slacking off, etc.

She clearly outlined roles and responsibilities for the team leaders.

Upon return, the coach asked for a recap, "Well, how did it go?" Without hesitation, one young man piped up: "What you shared last week made a huge impact on me. I really never thought of it that way before." Another young lady added, "I wholeheartedly agreed with everything you said, it all made perfect sense." A third student went further: "When you spoke to us, I was so moved I actually memorized several of your key points and takeaways."

Pleased with the responses, the coach replied, "OK great! So, each of you did what I said, correct?" After an awkward silence, one kid in the back muttered, "Nope, we didn't realize we were actually supposed to do anything."

What good would have resulted from the Israelites "being impacted by" possessing the land but failing to do anything about it, as opposed to them saying *"All that you have commanded us **we will do,** and wherever you send us **we will go.**"* (Joshua 1:16)

Or, in a New Testament case, the Twelve Disciples "agreeing with" or "memorizing" Jesus' commission, *"Go into all the world and preach the Gospel to all creation,"* then doing nothing about it? Instead, *"every day, in the Temple and from house to house, they kept right on teaching and preaching Jesus as the Christ."* (Acts 5:42)

In reality, today's Christian has become all too proficient in the **hearing** part of the Gospel equation; the **doing** part is another matter.

To see for yourself, take some time over the next week to observe how common it is for Christians to "be impacted by, agree with and memorize" without any "doing." Then record every instance when someone claims to be appalled at the sad spiritual state of our country, yet remains speechless when asked what they are doing about it. (And, by the way, don't be caught off guard to see your observations come full circle as you observe these same patterns in your own life.) The Bible teaches that our God is a long-suffering God. But don't push Him.

Which brings us back to Joshua and the key to his unrivaled success. To find the answer, let's return to Nike. Quite simply, God just told him what to do: *"Joshua arise, cross this Jordan!"* And he **just did it:** *"all Israel crossed on dry ground."* (Joshua 3:17)

It was not complicated. Yes, the Holy Land was theirs for the taking, but someone had to go get it. Pray that we would do no less.

Before proceeding, there is one practical note I'd like to call to your attention. Notice what God did after giving the go-ahead to cross the river? He waited. That's right, The Lord waited on Joshua and the priests to take the first step before He would act. Only after seeing ripples in the Jordan's waters from their toes touching it would God make His next move: *"It shall come about when the soles of the feet of the priests who carry the ark of the LORD, the Lord of all the earth, rest in the waters of the Jordan, the waters of the Jordan will be cut off, and the waters which are flowing down from above will stand in one heap."* (Joshua 3:13)

Perhaps He is likewise waiting to see ripples in that river presently blocking your path before He moves.

"We must strive to do ordinary things extraordinarily well." —Sister Catherine McAuley

---

In his book *Life of Excellence,* my friend Richard Simmons shares:

"At the first of every year, I now seek to make several small changes that will become permanent in my life. I have found that if I focus on just a few small changes, they create momentum, and it, in turn, impacts other areas of my life. You could almost say there is a ripple effect... if you want to have an exceptional life, a life of excellence, and truly reach the potential God has endowed you with; you must walk down certain paths that most people are not willing to walk down. However, when you do, it will make all the difference in the quality of your life and the legacy you leave behind."

In keeping within the context of The Relay, to help you walk—or, better yet, run—down "difference-maker" paths, I'll recommend three disciplines gleaned from the book of Joshua to start you on your way. Each will provide traction, like spikes on a runner's shoes, that will, like Scripture, *"direct you in the way of wisdom; lead you in upright paths; when you walk, your steps will not be impeded; And if you run, you will not stumble."* (Proverbs 4:11-12)

The three disciplines are: immerse yourself, give and take, and conquest by multiplication.

Immerse Yourself

When I was 12 years old, my friends and I would swim in the Black Warrior River that ran right beside our neighborhood in Tuscaloosa, Alabama. The most pleasant memories of my upbringing can be found in those days; it was a stage of simplicity I'll not soon forget.

We came up with a wide variety of games to bide the time. For example, who could jump the farthest off the banks, or who could stay underneath the water longest. I recall one game we played: a contest to see who could jump into the water without letting their head go under. You can imagine how meekly and mildly we must have approached the banks and how awkwardly we must have leapt in, trying not to go under. Looking back, it took more of an effort to not go under than it did to go in over your head.

Sometimes I think we approach the Precepts of God that way. Sure, we're plenty glad to seek out the Word's wellspring for momentary refreshment: lightly splashing our faces to cool off, letting our toes dabble on the water's edge or perhaps venturing up to our waists should a more deeply religious mood strike. But not too much. Heaven forbid that we get carried away. To come to the Word so meekly, mildly, reluctantly, is, in fact, not coming at all.

In opposition to the timidity described above, Joshua offered but one prerogative to his fellow citizens as they approached Scripture: **Immerse yourselves!**

Look no further than his opening remarks in Joshua 1:8: *"This Book of the Law shall not depart from your mouth, but you shall meditate on it day and night, so that you may be careful to do according to all that is written in it; for then you will make your way prosperous and then you will have success."*

Should the Hebrews ask, "How frequently should the Law be on our lips?" The simple reply, *"Immerse yourselves!"* "Well how many devotions should we have on The Law?" *"Immerse yourselves!"* "What role must the Law play when conquering the Land?" *"The land will not be conquered nor sustained apart from the Law. Therefore, immerse yourselves!"*

Allow yourself to become so immersed in the Word of God, synonymous with The River of Life, that you long to touch it and taste it as one dying of thirst longs to drink a sip of water. Even to the degree, you can barely think of anything other than how to attain it. Go ahead, dive in over your head. Never assume it runs only waist deep. As referenced in a previous chapter, I give my word the bottom will be nowhere in sight. Not even close.

Give and Take

The Christian religion is one of mutual give and take. Neither giving nor taking is more spiritual or important than the other. For any disciple of Jesus, the notion of giving, such as to give of oneself or giving to others, is naturally accepted as a major tenet of the faith. But the suggestion that we must take to the same degree as we give feels counterintuitive, if not outright wrong. And yet it is a truth validated by Scripture. Let's look at take first:

Picture yourself stranded on a raft far at sea, expanses of water surrounding you on every side. And yet, in the midst of all that water you would easily die of thirst unless you drank from a fresh water source; it is your only shot at survival.

This is likely the setting you find yourself in right now: a copy of the Bible is nearby. It is likely within arm's reach—on your phone, the bedside table, your desk. Its presence surrounds you like an ocean. If you are not careful, the threat of dying of spiritual thirst is no less real. Your soul, no less than your body, has genuine cravings and longings that can only be satisfied by God. And so it is imperative that you take to your soul a steady source of what the Bible calls *"Living Water"* to survive.

The Old and New Testaments are filled with allusions of water as fuel for life:

King David

"As the deer pants for the water brooks, So my soul pants for You, O God. My soul thirsts for God, for the living God." (Psalm 42:1-2)

"O God, You are my God; I shall seek You earnestly; My soul thirsts for You, my flesh yearns for You, In a dry and weary land where there is no water." (Psalm 63:1)

The Prophet Jeremiah

"For I will satisfy the weary soul, and every languishing soul I will replenish." (Jeremiah 31:25, ESV)

Jesus the Water of Life

"Blessed are those who hunger and thirst for righteousness, for they shall be satisfied." (Matthew 5:6)

"But whoever drinks of the water that I will give him shall never thirst; but the water that I will give him will become in him a well of water springing up to eternal life." (John 4:14)

"They will hunger no longer, nor thirst anymore; nor will the sun beat down on them, nor any heat; for the Lamb in the center of the throne will be their shepherd, and will guide them to springs of the water of life; and God will wipe every tear from their eyes." (Revelation 7:16-17)

The application here is straightforward: **You simply cannot give out what you're not taking in.**

Yet there's one stipulation: Just like the Holy Land, the Living Water is there for the taking. All you desire. But you can't just stand there and look at it. Like Joshua, you must go and get it! You must take it in!

Now let's look at the give. The point at which the horde of Israelites crossed the Jordan River was the city of Gilgal. Situated 67 miles due north of Gilgal lies the Sea of Galilee. This Sea was custom fashioned from eternity to serve as the perfect setting for the preaching and teaching of the Lord's

Anointed once He arrived. Its terrain of abundance was a fitting backdrop for the parables of Jesus: the good soil, the lilies of the fields, fishers of men, casting a wide net . . . all readily seen nearby as Christ spoke.

In the opposite direction, 21 miles due south of Gilgal, lies the Dead Sea. The landscape utterly desolate, barren, completely devoid of all signs of life. Other than salt, no resource can be found. And yet the same River Jordan that feeds the Sea of Galilee, fueling all its vibrancy and life, equally feeds the Dead Sea. What could possibly account for such a dramatic difference between the two? The answer is illustrative for our purposes: The Dead Sea only takes water in; it never gives anything back out. The Sea of Galilee not only takes in the Jordan's water, but flows it forward.

Likewise, in the Christian religion this mutual give and take makes all the difference. Gladly we take in the Gospel, but freely we are to give it out. It, too, is a matter of life and death.

Conquest by Multiplication

"God was so real to my father that He became real to me."
—Missionary John Paton

In the Kingdom of God, conquests and advances are not always decided on Earth's grandest stages (i.e., Moses v. Pharaoh, Joshua v. Canaan). Myriads are fought and won in arenas you'd least expect, with outcomes no less momentous. I'll share one story that best captures my intent with this chapter. It touches every point I've hoped to make, including meditating on God's Word, serving as a starting block to propel another forward, being impacted and doing something about it.

As its background, a large part of my ministry at The Center for Executive Leadership is coming alongside men at multiple stages of faith—from seekers, to believers, to seminary students, to pastors and everything in between. All under the heading, "Getting men into the Word and the Word into the world."

During one of my weekly Bible study groups for young fathers, nothing particularly stood out. So I was surprised to hear from one attendee afterward; his short text relayed an intense conviction about something that was shared, a dire need for him to change, and not much else. After exchanging a short volley of texts, we set lunch to discuss further. Curiosity getting the best of me, I looked back over my notes from that study I had titled, "Christian Maturity . . . The Great Separator." Wondering to myself what I'd said that could have made such a profound impact, I guessed at several powerful statements that had done the trick.

After being seated, the man wasted no time getting to the purpose of our meeting. He pulled out of his coat pocket a list he'd drawn up under two headings: "Shortcomings" was followed by an extensive list of items like putting hobbies before daughters, work ahead of wife, etc. "Next Steps" was followed by a line of question marks running the length of the page.

In other words, he had no idea what action steps to take to grow in Christian maturity.

"The impetus for it all," he explained while pulling an index card from his coat "stemmed from this one quote."

"Growth is the great separator between those who succeed and those who do not. When I see a person beginning to separate themselves from the pack, it's almost always due to personal growth." —John Maxwell

That was it. (Humbling enough, as they weren't my own words.) As we ended our conversation, I encouraged him to keep his chin up, as a father's race of a lifetime can't be defined by a series of missed strides. And I shared a few suggestions, with establishing a daily quiet time at the top of the list.

A week later, the young father emailed me the following:

George,

This will make you smile. This morning my daughter woke up early and saw me sitting on the couch reading my Bible and asked what I was doing. I shared that I was spending time with Jesus. She responded by asking, "can I sit with y'all?" That made my day and hope it makes yours as well!

This chapter began: "Having been trained under the tutelage of his mentor for years, Joshua had no problem picking up where Moses left off. A cleaner exchange between generations cannot be found in Scripture. This was as smooth as it gets."

That quiet exchange between father and daughter was an equally momentous, equally seamless passing of the baton.

"There are clubs you can't belong to, neighborhoods you can't live in, schools you can't get into, but the roads are always open." —Nike

The roads connecting this generation to the next are always open. It's important that you travel down them. If the up and coming are not being mentored by you, the question becomes, "Then who?"

"Therefore, my beloved brethren, be steadfast, immovable, always abounding in the work of the Lord, knowing that your toil is not in vain." (I Corinthians 15:58)

4

DAVID

The Paper Chase

"He gave His instructions to Israel. He commanded our ancestors to teach them to their children, so the next generation might know them—even the children not yet born—and they in turn will teach their own children. So each generation should set its hope anew on God." (Psalm 78:5-7, NLT)

A favorite saying of the Puritans was, "the father is the mirror by which the child dresses himself." This statement made a huge impression on a young father as he was walking through the snow with his 5-year old son. As he walked ahead, he looked over his shoulder to find his son following. With all the grace that he could muster, the young boy struggled to walk in the footprints his father had left behind. "When I saw this," he said, "I thought to myself, 'It is incumbent upon me to walk very straight, when this little fellow is already following in my tracks.'"

Since 1993 when Jesus first "laid hold of me," my greatest desire has been to live in relentless pursuit of God. Having had no predecessor's footprints to walk in, no baton of faith handed to me, no voice instructing, "this is how you do it, son, this is the way," I've struggled tremendously trying to make tracks of my own.

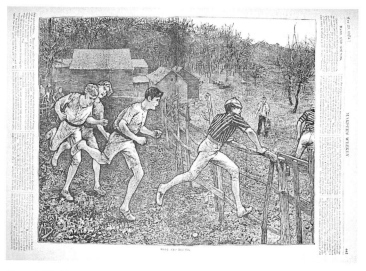

Harper's Weekly

Unquestionably, as a young father of two precious daughters, I already felt a degree of weightiness at the thought of charting a new course for my family. Something changed however on March 3, 2000, with the birth of my son James Miller. I distinctly recall the weightiness of responsibility bearing down a little heavier at the time, much like that father must have felt walking through the snow.

Later that evening in the hospital, as the steady flow of elated family members and friends tapered off, I found myself alone for the first time in the newborn viewing area. It was refreshing to pause for a few moments, just long enough to process the hurried events of the day, just long enough to peer through the partition glass observing my baby boy, only to be interrupted by a harrowing thought: "This little fellow is soon to be following in my tracks one day." My desire to relentlessly pursue Jesus remained unchanged, but the stakes of my faith race had unsettlingly climbed much higher. There I stood, momentarily caught in a spiritual no man's land, somewhere in between knowing who I was at present (an intimidated father delighting over his son) and who I aspired to be (a noble example that he and his siblings might one day be proud of). With no Godly model to lead and no solid bearings by which to navigate, I determined to exhaust the Scriptures and find a mentor whose life and legacy might serve as a "paper chase" to guide me through, to help me *"walk in the way of good men and keep to the paths of the righteous."* (Proverbs 2:20)

A paper chase, or "hare and hounds" was the early predecessor of cross-country running and originated in England at the Rugby School in 1837. To start the game, one student designated as the "hare" would take off running, leaving a trail of paper shreds along his route. After waiting 15 minutes, the remaining students, or "hounds," would begin their pursuit after the hare with his paper trail serving as "scent." While this game amused the schoolboys, its purpose was to prepare them for their futures as English gentlemen who hunted fox as a favorite pastime. The chase helped train these boys to become the men that they ought to be someday.

In my own chase, I looked to King David as my leader. This tender warrior and gentle shepherd knew what it was like to fail and fail badly, but had the resolve to get up and fight another day. His reputation is held in such high regard that Israel's flag, The Star of David, is flown in his honor. His highest accolade of all, however, one that no other person could ever claim, came directly from the mouth of our Almighty God: *"I have found David, son of Jesse, a man after My own heart; he will carry out My will in its entirety."* (Acts 13:22)

If such a man could carry out God's will so effectively, then maybe his legacy could serve as a type of paper trail for me to traverse and my children after me and their children after them. King David was exactly what I was looking for and is our next runner in *The Relay.*

Legacy Map

I had heard the phrase "visual learner" countless times growing up, but the concept was vague until a professor in a college communications class drew its meaning on a chalkboard. For the first time, I could actually see what I'd only heard and then it all made perfect sense, proving its own point: I'm a visual learner.

When it comes to Old Testament and New Testament History, maps that illustrate how Biblical narratives played out can be especially useful to visual learners. If you flip toward the back of your Bible, you'll likely find such maps replete with symbols, scales, keys and legends that delineate momentous exploits and travels in Biblical times that helped define our faith. You might see a map of the Patriarchs in Old Testament times that traces the fulfillment of God's promises to Abraham, Isaac and Jacob; or a New Testament map that diagrams the coming of Judaism's Messiah and the pathway His life traveled.

In light of how I most easily learn, paired with my desperate need to envision a healthy path to travel down, I decided to merge those two together by creating a map of my own that traced the life of King David. It's a Legacy Map, like a trail map that directs travelers which way they should go, or not go. Just as those maps in the back of my Bible allow me to visualize Biblical narratives in a clearer light, I created a map of my own tracing the life of King David so I might better understand the paths he took.

Currently, the map is taped to the back of a family picture that hangs on the wall in my office. Strategically placed directly across from my desk, it serves a purpose far greater than to map out in colorful form the start and finish, the peaks and valleys, the triumphs and trials of Israel's most heroic king. For me, it would be a waste to limit such a treasure trove of wisdom to paper alone. Rather, the greater purpose of this Legacy Map is to hover above and around me throughout the day as a constant reminder and challenge that, "it is incumbent upon me to walk very straight."

My Legacy Map is rudimentary and comprised of four components:

1. **PAPER TRAILS.** A series of routes David took over the course of his lifetime, some for the better, some for worse, some that are wise to follow, others that are not. "The Northern Heights" can be found toward the top of the map, symbolic of the high points David experienced in life. Lying just below is "The Southernmost Turn," representative of poor decisions he made. Little space separates North from South and intentionally so—a timeless reminder of just how few steps it takes to go from one to the other in so little time.

2. **DIRECTION.** We can learn much from the costly mistakes of another. I learn from David's; my kids learn from mine. On the other hand, much can be said for making new strides, like those David made to turn things around:

   We all want progress, but if you're on the wrong road, progress means doing an about-turn and walking back to the right road; in that case, the man who turns back soonest is the most progressive." —C. S. Lewis

3. **DESTINATION.** To one day be with Jesus in Heaven: *"Surely goodness and lovingkindness will follow me all the days*

of my life, and I will dwell in the house of the LORD forever."
(Psalm 23:6)

4. **LIFE LESSONS.** A handful of catchphrases I scribbled down similar to signposts, which became my version of citations like those used by mapmakers to help the viewer determine the use of the map for their own purpose. Two of David's life lessons have served me well, and I hope they will serve you well, too.

Brokenness Invites Usefulness

Do not sell the Gospel short. Jesus didn't just die for our sins; He died for our brokenness.

Israel's ascension to never-before-seen heights under King David's rule is unquestionable. History has made that case. Human nature makes the case that life's most tempting trailheads heading south start to emerge when we are at our heights. "Nearly all men can stand adversity, but if you want to test a man's character, give him power," observed Abraham Lincoln. His quote was likely a take on something David's son Solomon said centuries before: *"Pride goes before destruction, and a haughty spirit before stumbling."* (Proverbs 16:18)

At the apex of David's own power, strength and might, he started sliding down the wrong path, one small step at a time. Notice the snail's pace at which these Southern routes progressed, how harmless and small each step must have seemed to him at the time as he walked further and further into sin.

I would argue that men don't fall into sin, they slide. As C. S. Lewis observed, "Indeed, the safest road to Hell is the gradual one—the gentle slope, soft underfoot, without sudden turnings, without milestones, without signposts."

Put another way sin is—as defined by a sign I saw over a parking garage at Druid City Hospital in Tuscaloosa, Alabama—"Free In, Pay Out." It doesn't cost anything to get in. But you have to pay to get out. As the saying goes, "Sin will take you farther than you want to go, keep you longer than you want to stay, and cost you more than you want to pay." David was about to pay dearly.

As a pastor and I met over coffee, we were discussing II Corinthians 4:6-9:

> "For God, who said, "Let light shine out of darkness," made His light shine in our hearts to give us the light of the knowledge of God's glory displayed in the face of Christ. But we have this treasure in jars of clay to show that this all-surpassing power is from God and not from us. We are hard pressed on every side, but not crushed; perplexed, but not in despair; persecuted, but not abandoned; struck down, but not destroyed."

He proceeded to ask, "As jars of clay, we Christians have within us the light of Christ, which must shine to the outside world. How could that take place since light cannot shine through muddy clay?"

Before I could muster a guess, he answered his own question: "That's easy—the light can only be seen by the outside world as it shines through the cracks!"

In the case of King David, the light of his Heavenly Father shone through him brightest when he was at his weakest; in other words, through the cracks. Brokenness invites usefulness, or as Charles Swindoll put it, "It has been my observation over the years that the deeper the hurt, the greater the usefulness." And few broken men have ministered to me more than David. Nowhere is his brokenness more evident than Psalm 51.

Psalm 51:1-10

For the choir director. A Psalm of David, when Nathan the prophet came to him, after he had gone in to Bathsheba.

"¹Be gracious to me, O God, according to Your lovingkindness; according to the greatness of Your compassion blot out my transgressions. ²Wash me thoroughly from my iniquity and cleanse me from my sin. ³For I know my transgressions, and my sin is ever before me. ⁴Against You, You only, I have sinned and done what is evil in Your sight, so that You are justified when You speak and blameless when You judge. ⁵Behold, I was brought forth in iniquity, and in sin my mother conceived me ⁶Behold, You desire truth in the innermost being, and in the hidden part You will make me know wisdom. ⁷Purify me with hyssop, and I shall be clean; wash me, and I shall be whiter than snow. ⁸Make me to hear joy and gladness, let the bones which You have broken rejoice. ⁹Hide Your face from my sins and blot out all my iniquities. ¹⁰Create in me a clean heart, O God, and renew a steadfast spirit within me."

The historian would be hard pressed, even after the most extensive and exhaustive study of antiquity, to identify a sole case of a powerful ruler insisting that his subjects sing songs that highlighted his failures, not his strengths. That's exactly what David did when he addressed Psalm 51, *"For the choir director."* It would be the choir director's responsibility to put David's lyrics to music so that the entire realm of Israel would sing them aloud and learn from his sinful mistakes. Moreover, did you notice how he added the stinging title of the song himself: *"When Nathan the prophet came to him, after he had gone in to Bathsheba!"* And David was just getting started.

"There is something in humility which, strangely enough, exalts the heart, and something in pride which debases it." —Saint Augustine

Roman Emperor Marcus Aurelius, in his fight against pride, stationed a servant behind him to whisper in his ear, "you're only a man," when walking among those who were celebrating him. David needed no such external reminder; he was well aware of his limitations. Beginning in verse one with *"Be gracious to me O God,"* David's reasoning for why grace should be given him has but one basis: his full slate of transgressions. Instead of pleading for God's mercy based on all he has done right, he pleads for mercy based on all he has done wrong!

As you continue reading, notice how his brokenness intensifies with each succeeding verse.

❖ **VERSE 2** — *"Wash me thoroughly from my iniquity and cleanse me from my sin."*

❖ **VERSE 4** — *"Against You, You only, I have sinned, And done what is evil in Your sight."*

❖ **VERSE 5** — *"I was brought forth in iniquity, and in sin my mother conceived me."*

The crescendo of brokenness comes to a head in verse 10 when David uses the Hebrew word *bara*, which means "to create out of nothingness." On the surface, his word choice strikes us as intriguing, but there is so much more here than meets the eye. *Bara* was used exclusively to describe God's creative work in Genesis. Genesis 1:1, for instance, does not say *"in the beginning God formed, or God made, or God fashioned the Heavens and the Earth,"* as if He was working with raw materials, but rather, *"In the beginning God created ('bara') the Heavens and the Earth."*

You and I can form, make and fashion things, but only God can create from nothingness. The sole use of the word *bara* apart from the Creation account occurs in Psalm 51:10 as David exclaims, *"Bara in me a clean heart, O God!"* admitting that beneath his spiritual heart laid a vast chasm of nothingness, no raw materials with which God might work.

The brokenness of Psalm 51 always reminds me of a story by author Philip Yancey:

> Bill Watson was an alcoholic. Sober on his own for six months, he went out of town where a business deal fell through. Depressed, wandering a hotel lobby, he heard the familiar sounds of laughter and ice tinkling in glasses. He headed toward the bar thinking, "I need a drink." Suddenly a brand-new thought came to him, stopping him in his tracks: "No, I don't need a drink— I need another alcoholic!" Walking instead to the lobby telephones, he began the sequence of calls that put him in touch with another man by the name of Dr. Smith. Together these two men co-founded AA.
>
> — Philip Yancey, *Church: Why Bother*

All these years later since I first drew my map, the thought, "it is incumbent upon me to walk very straight," is no less harrowing. Then, as in now, the obvious realization is that I don't need to sin. But I must confess that from time to time I do need another sinner—not to minimize my wrongdoings, but to assure me that I, like King David, can get up to fight another day, that all has not been lost. Or in Winston Churchill's words, "Success is not final, failure is not fatal. It's the courage to continue that counts!"

The Afflictions of This Life Keep Our Affections on the Next

"Honesty, vulnerability and a good amount of courageous faith allows you to cry out in your bewilderment and not lose your belief in the process. These things allow you to wrestle your faith rather than lose it." —U2 lead singer Bono

"The road to holiness," said Dag Hammarskjold, "necessarily passes through the world of action." In my experience, "the road to holiness necessarily passes through the world of affliction."

King David not only passed through the world of affliction, but he seemed to reside there. This, I believe, accounts for his passionate longing for Heaven. According to C. S. Lewis, "If we find ourselves with a desire that nothing in this world can satisfy, the most probable explanation is that we were made for another world."

But do not be fooled: In no way did David perceive this life as a necessary evil to trudge through in order to make it to the next one. Rather, he was fond of his time here (browse the Psalms to see for yourself)—but not so fond as to make his love for eternity grow cold. In other words, the afflictions of this life kept his affections on the next.

All of which should give just cause to ask ourselves: Could it be possible God allows the present afflictions in my life to keep my affections on the next? Should I heed Paul's advice and *"consider that the sufferings of this present time are not worthy to be compared with the glory that is to be revealed to us?"* (Romans 8:18) Both are excellent questions to consider.

One of my all-time favorite quotes comes from Pastor Harry Reeder: "Be leery of the Christian who does not walk with a limp." He was referencing a story in Genesis 32 when Jacob wrestled with God throughout the night, refusing to quit until he received a blessing. The Lord granted Jacob's request as the dawn was breaking. In the process of literally striving with God, the Hand of God touched the socket of Jacob's hip, leaving him with a lifelong limp, which reminded him of the day he beheld his God.

King David had a limp of his own. To what degree his limp was brought upon himself is not the primary issue. The fact is, it left him spiritually debilitated, causing him to fall so low he eventually landed at the bottom of a pit, which is exactly where we find him as Psalm 40 opens:

> *"I waited patiently for the Lord; and He inclined to me and heard my cry. He brought me up out of the pit of destruction, out of the miry clay, and He set my feet upon a rock making my footsteps firm. He put a new song in my mouth, a song of praise to our God; Many will see and fear and will trust in the LORD."* (Psalm 40:1-3)

At the time of Psalm 40's composition, in order to retrieve water from a well, a pail had to be lowered to the very bottom of the well and then drawn back up. David likely had a specific well in mind, possibly one he used in his shepherding days to water his flocks. He borrowed that imagery to express just how deep he'd sunk underneath the heavy burden of affliction: to *"the bottom of the pit of destruction."*

Given this perspective through David's eyes, at rock-bottom looking up, just imagine how unfathomable it must have been to see the descent of God's hand from Heaven reaching so far down. To be rescued in such dramatic fashion made it impossible to withhold this testimony from others. *"I have proclaimed glad tidings of righteousness in the great congregation; Behold, I will not restrain my lips, O LORD, You know. I have not hidden Your righteousness within my heart; I have spoken of Your faithfulness and Your salvation; I have not concealed Your lovingkindness and Your truth from the great congregation." (Psalm 40:9-10)*

As an extra measure of grace, as only a Most Loving Father could fathom, David was allowed to retain his limp for the remainder of his life. His limp, while painful, did help in a number of ways. For one, it prevented him from veering too far off the path as he was prone to do: *"Before I was afflicted, I went astray, but now I keep Your Word."* (Psalm 119:67)

Second, it caused him to have a greater dependence on God's Word: *"This is my comfort in my affliction, that Your Word has revived me."* (Psalm 119:50) Third, David was able to minister to others with afflictions, not in spite of his limp, but because of it: *"The LORD is near to the brokenhearted and saves those who are crushed in spirit. Many are the afflictions of the righteous, but the LORD delivers him out of them all."* (Psalm 34:18-19) Fourth, I believe his limp was a veiled gift from God; veiled in that David may or may not have understood it as such. Again, I have an easier time seeing his affliction as a veiled gift than seeing my own afflictions as veiled gifts. But, according to definition, God's gifts are "a brand of giving that highlights the benevolent desire of the Giver," not the receiver.

Stated simply, God highlights Himself and brings glory to Himself through our afflictions. We may not always like it, but that is His way of doing things, and we have to trust He has our best interest in view.

"Blessed be the God and Father of our Lord Jesus Christ, the Father of mercies and God of all comfort, who comforts us in all our affliction so that we will be able to comfort those who are in any affliction with the comfort with which we ourselves are comforted by God." (II Corinthians 1:3-4)

In the early 1980s, three members of an Irish rock band were involved in a prayer group named Shalom. Many of the others in attendance failed to see how Christianity and rock music could possibly intersect and warned the musicians against making any attempt to combine them. Thankfully the three men rejected the unsolicited advice.

Several years later, as the rock band was nearing the end of a recording session for their third album, the lead singer scrambled to find a Bible to inspire a final song. He found what he was looking for in Psalm 40:

"We were being thrown out of the studio by the studio manager because we had overrun or something and we had one more song to do. We wrote this song in about 10 minutes, we recorded it in about 10 minutes, we mixed it in about 10 minutes and we played it, then, for another 10 minutes and that's nothing to do with why it's called '40.'"

—U2 Lead Singer Bono during a 1987 concert

Later, Bono recalled:

"'40' became the closing song at U2 shows, and on hundreds of occasions, literally hundreds of thousands of people of every size and shape of T-shirt have shouted back the refrain, pinched from Psalm 6: 'How long (to sing this song)? How long hunger? How long hatred? How long until creation grows up and the chaos of its precocious, hell-bent adolescence has been discarded?' I thought it odd that the vocalizing of such questions could bring such comfort—to me, too."

Personally, and somewhat prophetically as it relates to this chapter, God used Psalm 40 in my own life far more than anticipated. Beginning with U2's rendition that first introduced me to that portion of Scripture in high school, I've wrestled through many of its themes ever since—not exactly the type of carefree paper trail I initially envisioned leading my children down. Never would I have chosen a less-than-easy path to traverse in life, never, but obviously He did. And that's okay. He is a Good Father and promised to only give me what is best. At the very least, I take comfort knowing others, my children included, have one less reason to be leery of me as Pastor Reeder warned. And if in any way that allows them to know more of Jesus, then so be it. That's just fine by me; it really is.

CHAPTER 4

The End of the Chase (at least in part)

"Be strong, therefore, and show yourself a man. Keep the charge of the LORD your God, to walk in His ways, to keep His statutes, His commandments, His ordinances, and His testimonies, according to what is written in the Law of Moses, that you may succeed in all that you do and wherever you turn." (First Kings 2:2-3)

— *David's Legacy Letter to his son Solomon*

In the Fall of 2018, underneath the arch of the Walk of Champions in the Grove at Ole Miss, the time had come to bid final farewells. Apparently, some of what we as parents tried to instill in our son Miller had stuck: "Always give a man a firm handshake, be sure to look him in the eyes." How strange it was standing there giving a final congratulatory thumbs up while watching that young man walking away, down a new path he'd have to wander on his own. Today I'm able to recount the entire scene somewhat like a slow-motion picture reel in my mind. Could I stop the reel for a split second I would, just long enough to pause briefly and look over my shoulder as I had done some 16 years before:

> Early one spring morning in Pensacola, Florida, as was my normal routine, I headed across my lawn to retrieve the morning paper. As I browsed through the previous day's news, I caught a glimpse of some movement behind me. Without noticing that I was observing him, my son was leaping from one of my footprints in the dew to another. As my subtle grin turned into a broad smile, I asked Miller what he was doing. Without looking up, and without missing a beat, he replied, "nothing much, just jumping in your feet."

The Legacy Map was for me. The Legacy Letter below was for him.

For James Miller Shamblin,

You, my firstborn son, have been given a surname which is "Shamblin." Like any surname it comes with a legacy of one variety or another; there's a history behind it, there's a story to tell. Sometimes the legacy has followed the way of Christ, other times it has not. For several generations preceding us it seemed like the "Shamblin" legacy lost what it once held dear; it got off course.

As a husband, as a father, as a pastor and as a man, I have labored as hard as I've known how to make that name one my sons and daughters can be proud of. I've always appreciated you and your siblings being patient with me because, as I've shared many times, I'm blazing a new path in unchartered territory. I really didn't have a man of God to lead me down the path of how to love a woman like Christ loved the Church, or how to just hug my son and tell him how he brings me great delight while sincerely meaning it.

Forging ahead has not always been easy; far from it, in fact. There's always a lot to learn especially when looking back; errors that were made, situations handled incorrectly, more blunders than I'd hoped. But I am proud to say even now that I'm a Shamblin. I'd like to think I've worn the name fairly well. What's even more special though is being allowed, by the grace of Jesus, to see my oldest son wearing the name far better. That makes me smile even now as I'm writing this.

More importantly, though, than a surname is the name that matters most in this life, which is "Christian." As a follower of Jesus, as a Christian, Miller you must desire above all to do justice to that name, to wear it well.

With everything in the core of your being, live in such a God-pleasing manner that others might see and equally affirm "I know Miller, and one thing for sure, he loves Christ; he wears The Name well. Miller does justice to That Name."

As you enter your Freshman Year at Ole Miss, let me challenge you to keep hungering and thirsting for righteousness as you run hard after Precious Jesus. As both of us know, He's a good Savior, a reliable Savior. He is also your Savior and, as His follower, as a "Christian," and as a "Shamblin," you must wear the names well. Miller, keep doing justice to those names.

Peace,
Dad

The viewing room in the hospital, the early morning footprints in the dew, the final goodbye at college, 18 whole years, all within the blink of an eye. If brokenness invites usefulness, and I believe it does, I'd like to think I left some semblance of a paper trail to guide him—at least part of the way. And, if so, then that's okay with me. It really is.

What action steps can you take? I offer a special action step just for dads and a special action step just for moms.

TO DADS

Don't give fatherhood a go all on your own. Remember, you were not designed to run a lifelong race totally alone. You belong to a community that is much bigger than just you, and you need us as much as we need you. Pinpoint two men who can serve as a type of spiritual life coach for you. Write down the names of the two men who will proactively speak truth into every facet of your life: how to be a good daddy, how to best conduct yourself in business, how to make your wife feel cherished, how best to win over her affection repeatedly. Men who will meet with you on a regular basis and ask you to give them a progress report. Vow to contact each of the two men whose names you wrote down before the week is out. Request help by explaining how absurd it would be for any man to try and figure out all the above on his own. Trust me: the transparency will be well received.

TO MOMS

Consider shedding more light on your story to your children, and do so soon as the temptation to put it off will only grow with time. Age-appropriate, yes; gory details, no. Perhaps you've chosen to conceal or even lie about all the reasons why you walk with a limp. Please don't do that. It makes you not seem real. Young people have a keen knack for snuffing out your "do as I say, not as I did" mentality. You may think, "my kids won't open up and tell me anything in their world." Did you ever stop to wonder why?

Some decisions you made were more costly than you could have realized at the time. You were not immune to hurtful setbacks and situations that were beyond your control. If you've given yourself wholly to Jesus, don't forget to include these pivotal moments of reconciliation, renewal, redemption, and adoption in your story. When rolled together, these experiences have made you who you are. Start telling your personal story to your children and watch how they reciprocate.

"In the dust of defeat as well as the laurels of victory there is a glory to be found if one has done his best."
—Eric Liddell

5

JOSIAH

What Went So Terribly Wrong?

"Knowing the time . . . now it is high time to awake out of sleep: for now is our salvation nearer than when we believed. The night is far spent, the day is at hand." —Paul (Romans 13:11)

The church is asleep. Only a loud voice will awaken it from its slumber." Such was the somber state of Christianity in the 1730s, according to George Whitefield. Little did he know then that his would be that voice that God would use to awaken the 13 Colonies from their deep sleep. The dawn of the first Great Awakening had risen.

Rarely do American history books highlight the fact that the first American celebrity was not a movie star, nor a singer, nor any type of performer, but a Bible-believing evangelist from England named George Whitefield. During the course of his seven preaching tours in the New World, more than 80% of all colonists heard him preach at least once . . . in person! That's four of every five. Prior to his final departure for home, his farewell sermon at Boston Commons attracted more than 23,000 people—exceeding Boston's entire population.

As a direct result of the faithful preaching of God's Word by men such as George Whitefield, Jonathan Edwards, John

Wesley and others, untold scores of men, women and children were, in the language of the time, "quickened unto salvation" in Christ. The pews in New England's churches started filling to capacity, many overflowing into nearby fields. The Methodist ranks expanded so speedily that they soon ran out of pastors. The pews in their churches were full; the pulpits were empty. To remedy the problem, they developed a circuit-rider system whereby a single minister would fill multiple pulpits by traveling a circuit on horseback each Sunday.

At the same time, the Baptists grew westward stride-for-stride with the adventuring pioneers headed for the wild frontier. Considering that awakenings, by their very nature, don't slow down long enough for aspiring ministers to get adequate seminary schooling, the Baptists had no choice but to ordain lay ministers on the spot—laborers who were willing to work the fields by day and preach by night.

This religious fervor spilled over into the academic realm as well; the vast majority of universities established during that period were unabashedly founded on Biblical principles espoused by the Great Awakening. One college in Boston was particularly unapologetic about its primary goal: "The main end of a student's life is to know God and Jesus Christ."

Regrettably, over less time than one might imagine, that vibrant church once awakened from her slumber soon returned to sleep. Today, if you were to visit any of the Boston churches where George Whitefield preached, you might find a restaurant or department store or vacancy sign now occupies that space. But perhaps most telling of all, some are museums where you have to pay to hear what once happened there. And what about that college and its primary goal for students "to know God and Jesus Christ?" You now know it as Harvard, hardly a present-day bastion of Biblical Christianity.

All of which begs the question: What went so terribly wrong? Only one plausible explanation can be found: One generation failed to pass the baton on to the next.

God Clearing His Throat, thus Giving Himself Away

Throughout the Old Testament, a predictable pattern emerges of the Israelites sprinting toward God and His statutes one minute, then sprinting away the next. In a most stunning example, the Jews ran so far away and kept on running, to the point that eventually, not a single person could recall what the Torah was. Apparently, after decades of neglect, their Holy Scriptures were completely hidden from sight, buried deep within the inner recesses of what resembled a run-down museum—a place where amazing things once happened long ago. Despite repeated warnings, *"Beware that you do not forget the LORD your God by not keeping His commandments and His ordinances and His statutes"* (Deuteronomy 8:11), they forgot their God entirely. They dropped the baton.

Temple Restoration Begins

In its more glorious days, the Temple in Jerusalem was at the center of Jewish life. Exiled pilgrims from Earth's four corners flocked to it, vast armies waged wars over it, poetic Psalms were written about it. It was constructed as the venue whereby an Unblemished God chose to intersect with very blemished men. The Temple was to foreshadow greater things to come.

Over time, however, God's people sought to travel a darker path that led not toward Jerusalem but away from it. Many of the Levitical priests followed suit, and as they abandoned their posts of Temple maintenance, gross disrepair began to set in. The previous glory and majesty that filled God's Temple was all but gutted. In moments like this benefited by hindsight, certain verses we might have previously overlooked can give off new rings, such as 2nd Timothy 2:13 which teaches: *"though we remain faithless, He remains faithful."*

Solely as an act of His faithfulness, despite Judah's faithlessness, God placed on the throne of Judah an 8-year-old child named Josiah. At age 16, he *"began to seek the God of his father David."* (2nd Chronicles 34:3) At 20, he obliterated every pagan idol that littered his land. At 26, God planted within him a deep-seated desire to refurbish the Temple in Jerusalem. No sooner had the repairs begun than God allowed something long forgotten to be rediscovered: Himself. The Lord went far beyond *"being found by those diligently seeking Him"* (Proverbs 8:17) by more closely resembling, as German theologian Meister Eckhart wrote, *"a person who clears his throat while hiding and so gives Himself away."*

The story unfolds in 2nd Chronicles 34 as Josiah commissioned a massive team of officials, carpenters and workmen for the task of restoring the Temple. Among the debris, Hilkiah, the Highest Priest of the nation, accidentally happened upon a peculiar looking book he was unfamiliar with; it resembled some type of relic from the past. Unsure what had been discovered, Hilkiah consulted the scribe Shaphan for his expert opinion. One would naturally assume that a learned scribe could shed some light on any ancient manuscript, but it was not so. Equally unsure of what to do, Shaphan inquired of another—the King who ordered the repairs of the Temple in the first place. With the ancient discovery in hand, Shaphan concluded his briefing with King Josiah by casually telling the king a torah had been found; torah is Hebrew for book: *"Hilkiah the priest gave me a book."* (2nd Chronicles 34:18) Notice he did not say The Torah; rather, just some random book.

How preposterous it must have been, sounding more like the beginning of a bad joke: the sight of three of Judah's foremost religious leaders (a high priest, a scribe and a king) huddled around The Most Holy Torah of their religion, the Holy Bible itself, without any semblance of what it could possibly be, nor where it came from, nor what to do with it. All of which reminds me of something Martin Luther once said: "When everything is quiet, it could be a sign that the devil is the door-keeper of the Church and that the pure doctrine of God's Word has been lost."

It's safe to say, *"the people of God were quietly asleep. Only a loud voice would awaken them from their slumber."* Josiah's would become that voice, upending the entirety of nation that had long since forgotten their God, who knew not His Word.

Awakening in King Josiah

Initially, the workings of kingdom renewal began with Josiah alone. We might say the first movement of the Holy Spirit began on his throne. Unlike the ruler who once lamented, "I reform my country, and am not able to reform myself," King Josiah's reforms started within him first, beginning with the reconstruction of his own soul.

REFORM #1. Josiah's heart was *"tender,"* not hardened or stiff, and was therefore easily penetrable upon first hearing *"the words of the Law."*

"And Shaphan read from it in the presence of the king. When the king heard the words of the law, he tore his clothes." (2nd Chronicles 34:18-19)

REFORM #2. He was quick to blame his forefathers for their negligence, and rightly so, but he didn't get bogged down bemoaning their wrongs. Instead, his primary objective was what **he** the King needed to do about it: *"Go, inquire of the Lord for me…"*

"Go, inquire of the Lord for me and for those who are left in Israel and in Judah, concerning the words of the book which has been found; for great is the wrath of the Lord which is poured out on us because our fathers have not observed the Word of the Lord, to do according to all that is written in this book." (2nd Chronicles 34:21)

REFORM #3. The awakenings in Josiah were entirely authentic as evidenced by the Lord who *"knows the hearts of all men."* (1st Kings 8:39)

"Because your heart was tender and you humbled yourself before God when you heard His words against this place and against its inhabitants, and because you humbled yourself before Me, tore your clothes and wept before Me, I truly have heard you," declares the Lord." (2nd Chronicles 34:27)

The King was giddy over the recent discovery of a national treasure, reminding us of the Psalmist who wrote *"I rejoice at Your Word as one who finds great spoil."* (Psalm 119:162) All that was happening in him must have been truly exciting, but to quote Mark Twain: "To get the full value of joy you must have someone to divide it with." Josiah was soon to divide the great spoils with all.

Awakening through King Josiah

Humanitarian Bob Goff rightly observed:

"Something happens when you feel ownership. You no longer act like a spectator or consumer, because you're an owner. Faith is at its best when it's that way too. It's best lived when it's owned."

At this pivotal juncture in the 2nd Chronicles 34 story, the awakening was limited in large part to one person. Somehow, maybe intuitively, Josiah had the foresight to share the spoils of this remarkable discovery with his subjects, that they, too might own it, rather than being mere spectators or consumers. From that point forward, the revival would grow and spread *through him* reaching the outermost edges of his realm:

> *"³⁰The king went up to the house of the Lord and all the men of Judah, the inhabitants of Jerusalem, the priests, the Levites and all the people, from the greatest to the least; and he read in their hearing all the words of the book of the covenant which was found in the house of the Lord. ³¹Then the king stood in his place and made a covenant before the Lord to walk after the Lord, and to keep His commandments and His testimonies and His statutes with all his heart and with all his soul, to perform the words of the covenant written in this book. ³²Moreover, he made all who were present in Jerusalem and Benjamin to stand with him." (2nd Chronicles 34:30-32)*

The first way Josiah instilled ownership was that he brought along with him *"all the people, from the greatest to the least"* to worship with him at the house of the Lord, as opposed to worshipping alone. Second, rather than hoarding his recent discovery of The Torah and keeping it all to himself, he, as noted in 2nd Chronicles 34:30, *"made God's Word famous"* by reading it aloud to all of Jerusalem's inhabitants. Third, Josiah not only modeled an amazing display of reverence as he *"stood to it"* (2nd Chronicles 34:31) when The Torah was read, as if sitting were too casual, but he also called upon his countrymen to join him on the podium and "stand to it" as well.

"The pastor had best not do anything that the body itself could do. The pastor's primary task is to equip the body, not try to do everything for the laity. It is pride and an overwhelming need to control that causes the pastor to attempt to do the work of the entire congregation."

—Thomas Oden

In sum, the mighty work which God began in Josiah spread through him to the outer edges of his kingdom, allowing him to leave an amazing legacy behind: Josiah *"confirmed the words of the Law which were written in the book that Hilkiah the priest found in the house of the Lord. Before him there was no king like him who turned to the Lord with all his heart and with all his soul and with all his might, according to all the law of Moses; nor did any like him arise after him." (2nd Kings 23:25)*

Ensuring the Sacred Writings Never Have to be Rediscovered

"Voltaire, the famous French philosopher, was a brilliant atheist. He wrote a number of tracts deriding the Bible. He once made a very bold statement: 'One hundred years from today the Bible will be a forgotten book.' After Voltaire died, for nearly 100 years, his homestead was used as the book depository for the French Bible Society. They sold Bibles out of his house!" —Rick Warren

Thankfully, in that case, Voltaire was proved wrong. But at various times in given corners of the world it might have seemed as if he were right. There have been entire cultures that neglected the Bible to one degree or another, possibly as an oversight at first, but eventually allowing it to be thought of as nothing more than an ancient relic. It can happen quicker than you think, as the final story of this chapter will illustrate.

A pertinent question to ask ourselves is this: How do we as God's people as a whole keep from making the same mistakes as previous generations, like the generation that lost God's Word preceding King Josiah?

To take it one step further, how do we as believers keep our local churches from becoming museums similar to those in Boston where George Whitefield once preached in the first Great Awakening?

Or to press the issue to the front doorstep of your home, how can you individually ensure that the Sacred Writings you hold so dear will never have to be re-discovered by those who run after you?

Among myriad offensive and defensive measures that could be taken to safeguard God's Word from its three greatest threats—the world, the flesh and the devil—two in particular top the list: I call them **Entering His Visitation** and **Inviting Others into His Visitation.** Together they form a line of demarcation around The Scriptures, continually reminding us of its sacredness, while at the same time warning the Gates of Hades they will never prevail against it. (Matthew 16:18) We'll look at both in greater detail.

Entering His Visitation

"It is our duty and our privilege to exhaust our lives for Jesus. We are not to be living specimens of men in fine preservation, but living sacrifices, whose lot is to be consumed." —Charles Spurgeon

It's not possible for a modern museum to be built on top of an active fire. In Biblical times, the fire under the Temple altar had to be tended to continually; otherwise, the sacrifice would grow cold. In the same way, Christians are living sacrifices who must *"kindle afresh"* the flames of the Gospel within us lest our faith and our witness grow cold. (2nd Timothy 1:6)

"Unless the flame of love be kept bright and glowing, He will withdraw His support. He will not hold up an expiring lamp. The light of the Gospel is not extinguished but is removed from one place to another. If it has become dim or ceased to shine in one part of the Earth, it burns with brilliancy in another." —G. Rogers

The lesson for any disciple of Jesus is this: It is imperative to set aside ample time for personal devotion—to touch the floor with your face as you fall down to adore Him, to extend your hands high so as to reach His very throne room, to make melodies from whatever tune flows up from your heart—all of which combined generate more than ample wind to fan the flames of revival in your soul, preventing the embers there from ever-growing cold. The Bible defines these things as *"worship"*; or as I affectionately phrase it, **entering His visitation.**

One of the most gifted preachers of all time was Charles Spurgeon, who defined revival as "to kindle into a flame the vital spark which was nearly extinguished."

All revivals and awakenings the world has ever known were birthed and bathed in worship. A.W. Tozer exclaimed: "Listen to me! Practically every great deed done in the church of Christ all the way back to Apostle Paul was done by people blazing with the radiant worship of their God." Conversely, and not surprisingly, all revivals and awakenings that faded over time began to do so the minute worship was abandoned.

What exactly does **entering His visitation** mean? Allow me to paint the following picture:

Picture yourself going out for a run, along a scenic route perhaps, maybe an oceanfront or a beautiful valley. At a given point, as you are praying and thanking God for His goodness, you sense that you've run up on something far

"The Spirit and the bride say, "Come." And let the one who hears say, "Come." And let the one who is thirsty come; let the one who wishes take the water of life without cost."

greater than yourself. Stopping to stand in awe does have its place, as Wallace Stegner remarked while gazing at the Teton Mountain Range: "We need that wild country, even if we never do more than drive to its edge and look in."

However, I would contend, and I do believe sound theology backs me up on this, that God strategically placed those "far greater than yourself" stations at precise locations along your path; much like water stations set up for runners in a race. It's no coincidence that you happen to run upon them when thirsting the most. He did so with a far greater purpose than for you to contently stand on the edges looking in. How bizarre it would be to run past a water source without stopping to drink your fill? How much more bizarre it would be to run past The Messiah Jesus and The Holy Spirit as they call out to you: *"The Spirit and the bride say, "Come." And let the one who hears say, "Come." And let the one who is thirsty come; let the one who wishes take the water of life without cost."* (Revelation 22:17)

Should you heed the call and *"come,"* upon your entrance, that aforementioned "wild country" instantaneously becomes sacred ground on which you stand. For ground to become sacred, pews aren't necessary nor are church buildings mandatory. Jesus Himself taught that even the open air is conducive to worshipping *"in spirit and in truth."* (John 4:23) Wherever that place of meeting occurs between down here and up there, where His nearness comes closer as He invites us in, and we *"draw nigh"* unto Him, as a symbolic and fitting gesture you might feel inclined to remove your sandals as you stand in His presence. Now that's why I define worship as "entering His visitation."

In moments like these, something about being here on Earth doesn't feel quite right, and a type of homesickness overcomes me, leaving me to ask, "When will I be able to come back home?"

> "Have you never, in the dying embers of a Sunday night, rested your head on the pillow with wet eyes because the day of congregating in the presence of God does yet not last forever?"—Sinclair Ferguson

Inviting Others into His Visitation

"Where two or three have gathered together in My name, I am there in their midst." —Jesus

It's not enough to worship in solitude. You were created for community, and as you and your brothers and sisters worship together as a body, you will notice how something profound takes place with the addition of each new worshipper. What takes place exactly I'm not sure, but you can sense it when it happens. In the same way, every time a new convert is added to The Relay something unique and special occurs—much like strength in numbers—giving us a renewed sense of staying power or longevity or impact. Whether by witnessing or worshipping, each generation must actively replenish itself with the next generation; otherwise, the consequences can be disastrous.

You've heard the expression, "You'll know it when you see it." That same principle holds true of revival. During Spring Break 2018, my wife, Jill, and I led a team of 30 college students on a mission trip to Cuba with Reel-Life International. This was an opportunity to travel to the country that had previously been closed. The freedom to openly share the Gospel has remained closed ever since the Revolution of 1959; the original Constitution declared Cuba to be an atheistic state, although some positive steps toward religious liberty are currently being undertaken.

Starting at the airport in Havana before exiting the terminal, Jill and I independently kept getting this nagging sense that we were on the verge of some happening, something moving far beyond ourselves, but we didn't know what. On the third day of the trip, we loaded our bus and headed for Henequen, a small town about 40 kilometers away. Unbeknownst to us then, that nagging we sensed at the airport was only 40 minutes away.

Shortly after arriving, Jill's team split off to do door-to-door evangelism; her group consisted of two college students, a translator and Claudia, the local house-church member assigned to their team. Claudia hurriedly escorted them to meet with her son. Her hopes were high that maybe these Americans might have success leading her son's wife Marcia to Christ. After exchanging pleasantries, one of the students asked a simple question, "Are you a Christian?" "No" came Marcia's straightforward reply. Which incidentally speaks to the refreshing directness when witnessing in Cuba, where a "no" is self-evident and a "yes" presupposes the cost has already been counted in making such a profession. Conversion in that country likely entails the loss of one's job, the loss of one's status in society, one's well-being, etc. Communism has a way clarifying who's in the faith and who's not.

When asked if she would be open to hearing the Gospel,

Marcia was gracious, saying they could share if they like. Even though she appreciated the good influence Christianity had on her family and community, she had no personal interest in becoming a follower herself. Undeterred, Jill talked about Jesus and His message for the next 30 minutes. Not once did Marcia give any indication she was open to the faith.

Seemingly out of nowhere, the humbly decorated living room was transformed into a most grand and elaborate house of worship: a place whereby an Unblemished God intersected with blemished men, a foreshadow of what was about to come. (Isaiah 32:18)

The Holy Spirit's presence thickened. Marcia's demeanor grew different; where once no life in her eyes could be detected, life and light appeared, and spiritual walls and barriers were collapsing all around. Then came what Jill could only describe as a "very distinct moment"—the exact point in time when Marcia transitioned from unreceptivity to receptivity, so real that Jill felt as if she could reach out and physically touch it. Reiterated by missionaries fortunate enough to have experienced revival ("you'll know it when you see it") Jill saw it, having the discernment to come to a dead pause and stop talking . . . the silence only broken when she extended the three-word invitation, "Are you ready?"

Marcia did not need Jill to clarify what she meant by "are you ready?" Marcia knew; they all knew. The Holy Spirit is well known to work that way. Her response was simple, but no less Heaven-altering: "Yes. I am ready."

The subsequent outflow of tears was not a certain indicator of her heart, but a good indicator. Tears mark revivals above every other emotion. It's no wonder the Puritans earnestly prayed "for the gift of tears." As it turns out, Marcia's "yes, I am ready" came at a high cost: Any time a high-ranking Communist official like her defects to follow a humble Galilean, it never sits well with the powers that be.

Later that evening, our team huddled up to debrief on all that happened throughout the day. Before long, it became apparent that the more we attempted to put into words *"what we have heard, what we have seen with our eyes, what we have looked at and touched with our hands, concerning the Word of Life,"* (1st John 1:1) the more intimacy of our experience was lost.

As for that nagging sense that we were on the verge of some happening, something moving far larger than ourselves ... "Nobody told you?" one of the translators later inquired. "Oh, they should have mentioned it. All seven pastors you worked with today, plus their spouses, plus every member of all seven churches, have been fasting and praying for your team ever since you landed three days ago. Just thought you would like to know."

Our Cuban brothers and sisters continue to delight themselves in the Lord today, in the sweetest of ways, in the sweetest of seasons I have ever witnessed. They have been more than hospitable to those of us just happy to stand on the edges looking in, granting us full access instead: a mutual exchange of visitations. The fact that the once-present Christian influence is now reappearing in that wonderful country with the witness of those like Marcia brings great hope for the future.

It also impresses me in several ways. For one, if we are not careful in our own country, could the same thing happen under our watch?

Finally, like a staggered start in a relay where runners begin at different points on the track, you may become discouraged about where you were on the track when you got the baton—maybe another delayed getting it to you on time, or you were handed the wrong baton, or you possibly received no baton at all—take heart because there is some amazing news for you: It only takes one person to stand between Exodus 20:5 and Exodus 20:6. And you can be that person!

Exodus 20:5 says: *"I, the LORD your God, am a jealous God, visiting the iniquity of the fathers on the children, on the third and the fourth generations."*

The Israelites in Josiah's day could attest to how heavily the gravity of generational sin weighs one down, even in the third and fourth generations. However, Josiah realized that just because his forefathers dropped the baton, and subsequent generation after generation after generation handed off false batons or no baton at all, there's nothing that said he had to take what was given. In other words, it doesn't have to be that way!

On the opposite end of the spectrum, look to Exodus 20:6, where The Lord promises to shower *"lovingkindness to thousands, to those who love Me and keep My commandments."*

Notice that the lovingkindness God spread on behalf of one person who loves Him doesn't stop with the third and fourth generations; it is extended to thousands!

Only one runner stands between Exodus 20:5 and Exodus 20:6.

It takes one runner to reverse even the most severe of generational curses. Like Josiah, like Whitefield, like Marcia— **you be that one person!** You be that loud voice to upend the entirety of a nation from their slumber so they, too, can begin crying out to the Living God.

6

JESUS

The Words You Placed in My Hands,
I Have Placed in their Hands

"The one who listens to you listens to Me, and the one who rejects you rejects Me; and he who rejects Me rejects the One who sent Me." (Luke 10:16)

There's one short scene in the movie *The Perfect Storm* where a deckhand asks the captain (George Clooney), "So, what are you so happy about?" To which the captain replies, "You just caught me on a good night. I'm doing what I was made to do—and I've got a feeling I'm going to do it even better this time."

The captain packed his entire goal in life, his ultimate mission and even his purpose for being on Earth into one short sentence—a feat many have failed to achieve in an entire lifetime. This is a feat many have failed to realize in an entire lifetime. Many people live their full lives without realizing their purpose. As a fisherman and as a captain he believed he was doing what he was made to do—he knew why he was here on this Earth.

Jesus made it unquestionably clear why He came to Earth and what His purpose was. And yet today, His followers seem to have a hard time succinctly stating why He visited us as One of us.

The goal of this chapter is to first identify why Christ came, then determine what He wants you to do, so then you can begin the process of aligning your purpose with His purpose.

How would you answer the question, "Why did He come here?" Your answer might be something like, "He came to die for our sins" or "He came to save us" or "He came to give us life." While each of these statements is true, by His own account, Jesus stated in no uncertain terms precisely why. According to Jesus, His coming had everything to do with His Word.

He came to preach the Word.

He came to proclaim Good News.

He came to testify to the Truth.

The New Testament never mentions anything about Jesus running, much less participating in a relay. He cannot be relegated as One among many. Jesus has stood, and always will stand, single and alone.

This does not mean, however, that He carried out all of His Father's will to the exclusion of those who would follow Him. Quite the opposite. He invites us into His work through the Holy Spirit's power that we might go and do likewise. As you're about to see, the goal was not to win a race . . . but to win the world.

This is What I Came For

In the Gospel according to Mark, Jesus set a dizzyingly fast pace of ministry over a short span of time. Mark's habit was to preface Jesus' flurry of activities with the word "immediately." He used this word 41 times to show the urgency with which Jesus' mission began, causing the reader to try and pause long enough to catch his or her breath. In the midst

of it all—baptisms, healings, calling disciples, casting out demons—we must be careful to not rush past Mark 1:38. It was
the first of three examples of why Jesus came to Earth as
expressed by Him in His own words: *"let us go somewhere else to
the towns nearby, in order that I may preach there also; for this is what
I came for."* Simple enough.

One Anointed to Preach

The hour belonged to Him and he commanded the moment, as if He'd spent an eternity waiting in earnest until
the summons was issued. Ascending the pulpit, the small-
town preacher always knew, as far back as He could recall
(30 years ago, in fact), that God had placed "the call" on His
life to administer the Gospel. While other youngsters envisioned what they wanted to be when they grew up, how they
might earn a respectable living by following in the footsteps
of their fathers, He aspired for more Heavenly ideals, forfeit-
ing whatever necessary to make an everlasting impact—in
fact, to alter history.

The pressure of returning home to proclaim that first sermon must have been intense. Those who knew Him growing
up predicted He'd amount to little, especially with no proper
schooling to speak of. It was the wise sages, after all, who
said, "No prophet is welcome in his hometown." The assem-
bled congregants eagerly anticipated His opening theme. Ru-
mor had it He'd worked on this particular message for the
better part of 30 years. They'd learn soon enough.

An attendant in the sanctuary meticulously unrolled the
sacred parchments, placing the ancient scroll in the Preacher's palm and turning to a selected reading from Isaiah the
Prophet. How at home that scroll must have felt in that hand.
The divine irony lost on all. The oracles handcrafted by Him
from eternity returning back into His hands! At long last, the

Word of God had come full circle, secure once again in its rightful Owner's possession.

Their fellow Nazarene began by exclaiming: *"THE SPIRIT OF THE LORD IS UPON ME, BECAUSE HE ANOINTED ME TO PREACH THE GOSPEL TO THE POOR. HE HAS SENT ME TO PROCLAIM RELEASE TO THE CAPTIVES, AND RECOVERY OF SIGHT TO THE BLIND, TO SET FREE THOSE WHO ARE OPPRESSED, TO PROCLAIM THE FAVORABLE YEAR OF THE LORD."* (Luke 4:18-19)

Surely, one would assume, the response to this incredible reading and sermon must have been favorable. Could they have just witnessed the beginnings of a hometown hero who proved all doubters wrong, especially the sages once regarded as being so wise?

> *"And all the people in the synagogue were filled with rage as they heard these things; and they got up and drove Him out of the city, and led Him to the brow of the hill on which their city had been built, in order to throw Him down the cliff."* (Luke 4:28-29)

All this furor because they didn't like what He had to say and how He said it. It does make one wonder that if the opposition to Jesus' inaugural sermon was so fierce, what would happen after He delivered His last? In three short years, all would find out.

For This I Have Been Born

Napoleon once observed that millions of people would be willing to die for Jesus, who founded his spiritual empire through love, yet none would be willing to die for Alexander (or Napoleon himself), who founded an empire through force. He saw in this contrast a convincing argument for the divinity of

Christ, saying: "I know men, and I tell you, Christ was not a man. Everything about Christ astonishes me. His spirit overwhelms and confounds me. There is no comparison between Him and any other being. He stands single and alone."

Jesus stated His mission for coming to Earth at the beginning of His public ministry; what did he say at the end? To find the answer, let's turn to the most perplexing exchange ever witnessed in a court of law between the highest Roman Ruler in the Judean region, Pontius Pilate, and the Highest Ruler in the cosmos, Jesus of Nazareth. Pilate, like Napoleon, ruled his temporal empire by force. Christ ruled His spiritual empire by love. Confounded, Pilate asked, *"So, you are a King?"* The incomparable Christ, standing single and alone, replied, *"You say correctly that I am a King. For this I have been born, and for this I have come into the world, to testify to the truth."* (John 18:37)

The implication in saying *"to testify"* in 30 AD meant full disclosure; one would share his account publicly holding nothing back. Here we have the fully Man and fully God Jesus withholding His defense, standing in silence before Pilate. Having never withheld His testimony to save others, He did so then, thereby unwilling to save Himself. *"Like a lamb that is led to slaughter, and like a sheep that is silent before its shearers, So He did not open His mouth."* (Isaiah 53:7)

Had the Lamb of God not remained silent, how tremendously our world would have suffered. How tremendously you and I would have suffered, too. In the face of Jesus withholding His testimony before Pilate to set convicted criminals free, how could we, in turn, withhold that same testimony from others who share our same plight?

On a personal note before going further: Should the occasion arise that I could read Jesus' exchange before Pilate with no emotional response, that's the signal for me to ease out of my profession. Like the time my daughter Sydney was turning the pages of her picture Bible, inquiring during the story of Jesus' trial, whipping and execution: "Mommy, why do I have water in my eyes? Why were they so mean? He didn't do anything wrong. Why did they do such a mean thing?" I hope to always ask myself the same.

"Everything about Christ astonishes me. His spirit overwhelms and confounds me. There is no comparison between Him and any other being. He stands single and alone." —Napoleon Bonaparte

---

It's All About Jesus and His Word

Jesus made it unmistakably clear that His mission in life was to preach the Word, to proclaim the Good News and to testify to the Truth. But some might ask, "What does testifying to the truth have in common with preaching the Word?"

According to John 17:1, *"Truth"* and *"Word"* are synonymous: *"sanctify them in the Truth; Your Word is Truth."* Furthermore, Jesus Himself is inseparably linked to His Word: *"If you abide in Me, and My Words abide in you, ask whatever you wish, and it will be done for you."* (John 15:7)

Therefore, you cannot have One without the other. Regardless which term you pull out of Scripture's 66 books (precept, testimony, command, truth, law, Gospel, Word) the meaning of each is always the same. It's all about Jesus. It's all about His Word.

An Invitation Into

While seeking solace from the world in the Holy Bible, the 16th President of the United States, Abraham Lincoln, reflected: "I am profitably engaged in reading the Bible. Take all of this book that you can by reason and the balance by faith, and you will live and die a better man. It is the best book which God has given to man." Amen and Amen!

Certainly, God did give mankind the Bible as the greatest of gifts, as Lincoln believed. But have you ever considered the path that this best of books had to travel over thousands of years to reach Earth's remotest corners, let's say, in this case, the Oval Office? The Holy Land and Washington, DC, are 5,897 miles apart; the latter did not exist until July 16, 1790, and the two are separated by previously impenetrable mountain ranges and unnavigable bodies of water. And yet, Christ's proclamations in written form ultimately found their way from one to the other. How could that be? How?

To find the answer we need look no further than the road map Jesus laid out for His disciples in the Upper Room of Peter's mother-in-law's house. Gathered together in a loft, just moments before His impending execution, foot-washings, the last Passover and the first Lord's Supper all taking place, The Messiah extended an invitation "into."

"An invitation into what?" some might ask. He extended an invitation into the continuation of His work and mission to His disciples. That invitation for any who might follow Him has not changed since.

Thanks to John's account of what transpired behind the Upper Room's closed doors, you and I are able to slip in unnoticed right behind the Disciples and overhear what Jesus was saying to them. John also gives us the tiniest glimpse of what the world might have looked like as seen through the lens of Christ; he was the one, after all, leaning against the breast of his Savior, listening to Him speak while viewing the outside world. Even more, thanks to John, we're able to listen in on a very intimate conversation between Father and Son as Jesus prays on behalf of His disciples, *"the words You placed in My hands, I have placed in their hands (John 17:8) . . . sanctify them in the truth; Your Word is truth . . . as You sent Me into the world, I also have sent them into the world."* (John 17:17-18)

In Biblical times, "giving" meant "give one the hand." Thus, the very Torah God placed in Jesus' palm, Jesus in turn placed in the Disciples' palms, signifying a continual succession or "changing of the hands" of God's Word from one generation to the next.

Jesus' prayer is like a perpetual relay in which the baton never ceases to be exchanged; beginning with God entrusting the Word to Jesus, then Jesus entrusting the Word to the twelve Disciples, commissioning them to *"Go therefore and make disciples of all the nations, baptizing them in the name of the Father and the Son and the Holy Spirit, teaching them to observe all that I commanded you; and lo, I am with you always, even to the end of the age."* (Matthew 28:19-20)

Knowing that Biblical words are often packed with layers of meaning, why should anyone be surprised that our Great God chose to use the word 'go' to signal the beginning of the Disciples' race of faith, which means *"to transfer something from one destination (port) to another?"* Or how about *"to make disciples,"* which precisely means *"helping someone to progressively learn the Word of God to become a matured, growing Christ-follower."* (Strong's Concordance)

...why should anyone be surprised that our Great God chose to use the word 'go' to signal the beginning of the Disciples' race of faith, which means *"to transfer something from one destination (port) to another?"*

As if that weren't enough, we've got *"teaching them"* for extra measure. Of the 220 usages of *"teaching them"* in the New Testament, almost every single one refers to teaching the written Word of God.

When taken together, that's your explanation as to how the Word traveled from Jerusalem to the White House and beyond. The Great Bible is unhindered by barriers and disrespects boundaries. It will outlast every single thing you now behold—as Jesus put it, *"Heaven and earth will pass away, but My Words will not pass away."* (Mark 13:31)

Just as Moses transferred the Word to Joshua, Elijah to Elisha, David to Solomon, Paul to Timothy, Jesus transferred the Word to the Disciples before His departure from this Earth. The biggest difference from the above examples: all were equals. Jesus, however, was the Sole Superior handing off to 12 inferiors. He, as the Divine, handing off to humankind cannot be relegated as One among many others in The Relay. This by no means undermines the authority of His Disciples, because Jesus elevated their role as an extension of Himself; He empowered them as His ambassadors with the full backing of Himself, even to act and speak authoritatively on His behalf.

Paul, for one, would wholeheartedly adopt the role: *"He has committed to us the Word of reconciliation. Therefore, we are ambassadors for Christ, as though God were making an appeal through us; we beg you on behalf of Christ, be reconciled to God."* (2nd Corinthians 5:19-20)

According to one pastor's definition:

"The primary responsibility of an ambassador is to accurately represent and advocate for their home country's goals while abroad. In order to do this, they have to be thoroughly acquainted with their country's and ruler's policies, thoughts, and which outcomes are favorable or unacceptable. Similarly, we have to have a full, working (that means practical and useful) knowledge of God's plan—what has brought us to this point in history, how He plans to accomplish His end goal, and what our role is and will be—in order to be effective ambassadors for God and Christ on Earth."

—BeStirredNotShaken.com

All of which reminds me of a story a friend shared about her time in prison ministry: Each time she arrived at the prison, she had to present her credentials before she could enter. On one occasion, she had her driver's license but had misplaced the accompanying ID card of the ministry she represented. A kind guard made a one-time exception by filling out a temporary pass. Once past the checkpoint, my friend chuckled; in the blank space indicating who she was representing, the guard had written "God."

The purpose for any Christian ambassador, whether an initial ambassador in 30 AD or an ambassador in the 21st century, must have as his end goal preaching, proclaiming and testifying to the Word, thereby begging this lost world to *"be reconciled to God."* Therefore, for those who are Christians, you have no choice but to go and do likewise.

The next time a friend or coworker or Sunday school teacher invites you to **go** with them on a short-term mission trip, or to participate in an inner-city ministry, or serve at a local nursing home, you are free to reply "yes" or "no" as you wish. But, whatever you do, please don't respond by saying, "Let me pray and see if the Lord would have me go." He's already made it clear in Matthew 28:19 that as His ambassador, you are to "go." The only remaining option you're left with is to ask, *"Lord, is there any reason why You would have me stay?"* Which leads to, *"therefore, what must we do?"*

Go and Do Likewise

"Without meaning, nothing else matters. With meaning, everything else falls into place."— *Austrian neurologist, psychiatrist and concentration camp survivor Viktor Frankl*

An executive headhunter recounted to author and evangelist Josh McDowell a perspective-altering conversation he once had:

"When I get an executive that I'm trying to hire for someone else, I like to disarm him. I offer him a drink, take my coat off, then my vest, undo my tie, throw up my feet and talk about baseball, football, family, whatever, until he's all relaxed. Then, when I think I've got him relaxed, I lean over, look him square in the eye and say, 'What's your purpose in life?' It's amazing how top executives fall apart at that question. Well, I was interviewing this fellow the other day, had him all disarmed, with my feet up on his desk, talking about football. Then I leaned up and said, 'What's your purpose in life, Bob?' And he said, without blinking an eye, "To go to Heaven and take as many people with me as I can.' For the first time in my career, I was speechless."

Clearly, that executive got it . . . his life purpose extended farther than himself, an unselfish realization found by few. Once you figure out His purpose in coming to Earth and what He wants to give you who follow Him, then you must begin to align your purpose with His purpose.

Seeing that He came to preach the Word and testify to it, as one of His, what must you do? Go and do no less.

Mark Twain said, "The two most important days in your life are the day you are born and the day you find out why." In a Christian context, we could say two most important days are the day you were born again and the day you figure out why you were born again. If you've experienced one without the other, here's a claim you can make your own: "I'm where I am at this moment in time because Jesus has entrusted me with the continuation of what He started until the Earth's four corners have been reached."

As the Apostle Paul quoted from Isaiah, as Christ had done earlier, *"How then will they call on Him in whom they have not believed? How will they believe in Him whom they have not heard? And how will they hear without a preacher? How will they preach unless they are sent? Just as it is written, "how beautiful are the feet of those who bring Good News of good things!"* (Romans 10:14-15)

Do not think for a second that these directives were given to a select few way back when and have little implication for you. Quite the opposite. **You are every bit as called to testify to others as others testified to you.**

A missionary to Africa told how he once gave a new convert a copy of the Bible. When the two met months later the Bible was torn to shreds with most of its pages ripped out. Frustrated, the missionary exclaimed, "I thought you treasured the Bible I gave you and would handle it with great care." The man replied, "It is the finest gift I ever received; it is such a wonderful book that I gave a page to my father and a page to my mother then I gave a page to everyone in my village."

That new convert's relay had already begun. Early in his race, he went from being a mere disciple (one who learns) to an apostle (one who is sent). His life's purpose was to simultaneously run for God's glory while urging loved ones to join him in the race.

If you've not made that same move from disciple (one who learns) to apostle (one who is sent), the time is now. Be bold by offering up a prayer of discomfort in your role as a disciple until you transition into an apostle. C.S. Lewis said, "I didn't go to religion to make me happy. I always knew a bottle of

Port would do that. If you want a religion to make you feel really comfortable, I certainly don't recommend Christianity."

For any who are Christians, take comfort knowing that your unique gift set was custom-tailored by the Holy Spirit to perfectly empower you to carry out God's call on your life. Oh, that you might abound in sharing, not hoarding, your gifts. Attune your ears to humanity's current plight that wails in desperation to hear but one Word of Good News (*"for the anxious longing of the creation waits eagerly for the revealing of the sons of God."* (Romans 8:19) Yours must be that word. Pray now that insights into Jerusalem's landscape behind Paul's reference *"how beautiful are the feet of those who bring good news of good things"* would press you to action.

For thousands of years, the inhabitants of Jeru-Shalom (literally the city of Shalom or peace) knew anything but peace. Under the constant threat of invasion, watchmen were situated on the surrounding mountaintops. The populace didn't have a clue that watchmen existed until danger became imminent, at which time a flag was flown by day or a fire was lit by night announcing bad news. Never in the history of the world's most holy city did watchmen announce Good News. The Prophet Isaiah, writing some 700 years before the time of Paul, foresaw a proclamation of peace where the watchmen would announce, for the first time ever, Good News once Israel's long-awaited Messiah had arrived:

> *"How lovely on the mountains Are the feet of him who brings good news, Who announces peace, And brings good news of happiness, Who announces salvation, And says to Zion, 'Your God reigns!' Listen! Your watchmen lift up their voices, They shout joyfully together; For they will see with their own eyes When the LORD restores Zion. Break forth, shout joyfully together, You waste places of Jerusalem; For the LORD has comforted His people, He has redeemed Jerusalem. The LORD has bared His holy arm In the*

sight of all the nations, That all the ends of the earth may see The salvation of our God." (Isaiah 52:7-10)

The time has come for you, oh, ambassador of Christ, to run your race along the watchtower, waving your flag by day, kindling your fire by night, preaching great news. You, as a preacher with your own unique pulpit, are as equally endowed with the high calling of announcing good news as those watchmen were in Jerusalem, or as all those Christians in Rome were to whom Paul was speaking.

But you might object: "I'm no ambassador! I'm no watchman! And I'm certainly no preacher!"

In actuality, the "preachers" Paul wrote to included *"ALL who are beloved of God in Rome."* (Romans 1:7) Paul's point was this: Whether young or old, trained or untrained, male or female, rich or poor, each Christian has a pulpit from which he or she must preach.

Which begs the questions: "Which pulpit or which platform have you been given? Is any Good News currently being announced there?"

The people in your immediate sphere of influence are 100 times more likely to receive the baton extended from your hand than any other, including your ministers. *"How then will they call on Him in whom they have not believed? How will they believe in Him whom they have not heard? And how will they hear without a preacher? How will they preach unless they are sent? Just as it is written, how beautiful are the feet of those who bring Good News of good things!"* (Romans 10:14-15)

Now that's what purpose is supposed to look like. *"He who prepared us for this very purpose is God."* (2nd Corinthians 5:5)

Be Forewarned

The Bible includes many running analogies, as we've discussed, but for those readying to wave banners of Good News to win a hostile world, please keep these four advisements in mind:

FIRST, do not mistake humanity's dire desperation to hear Good News to mean that everyone will be glad to hear it from you. Far from it. Remember the response to Jesus' sermons. The light His truth exposed their darkness, and nobody ever likes to be exposed. I was furious the first time I was told how big my sin problem was and how only a perfect Savior could rescue me from it. I'm happy my friend loved me enough to speak plainly. He did not quit because of my resistance. That conversation changed my life. Expect resistance; you will encounter it quickly. But do not quit in the face of it. Rather, love others enough to keep on speaking the truth in love.

SECOND, never assume all "Christians" or "churchgoers" will be allied with your cause. History shows the most severe hostility encountered by every Gospel growth spurt came from within, meaning "churchgoers," 100% of the time. It's like friendly fire during battle, taking shots from people you assumed were on the same side; by far the cruelest and most hurtful assault of all. So if a close friend or associate, quite possibly a fellow church member, tells you to "dial this religious thing back a notch," or "it'd be best to keep the Bible thumping to a minimum," don't let it get you down. It happens all the time. I picked those expressions because I've said them myself. Receive any and all pushback and naysaying as a golden opportunity to practice the message you just preached by exhibiting grace, love, patience, kindness and joy. Sounds a lot like Christ, huh?

THIRD, the adversary will be displeased to learn that a banner-waving foot soldier of Christ, like you, has ventured into his domain. The evil one, as Paul called him, has a limited number of fiery darts in his arsenal. Surely kept in reserve, only to be aimed at those on the frontlines wreaking the most havoc in his, the devil's domain. Suit up now by 'putting on the full armor of God, so that you will be able to stand firm against the schemes of the devil." (Ephesians 6:11)

FINALLY, no matter how brutal the battle becomes as you share the Good News, you must keep the field. The Battle of Eylau in 1807 was a furious two-day conflict between Napoleon and the Russian Army, in which 50,000 soldiers died. Since both parties claimed victory, one professor inquired, "What then is the historian to do?" To which an astute student replied, "Why, he must inquire, who kept the field?" After the Battle of Eylau, it was the French who kept the field while the Russians fled.

After the dawn sets on this generation, may future historians survey the landscape declaring you were the one who kept it.

7

JOHN

The Apostle of the Word

"The Bible is alive, it speaks to me; it has feet, it runs after me; it has hands, it lays hold of me." — *Martin Luther*

In his book *Reaching for the Invisible God,* Philip Yancey references the sci-fi movie *Contact,* where Dr. Ellie Arroway (played by Jodie Foster) "lounges against the Very Large Array radio dishes day after day, night after night, until one day a distinctive pattern of sound crackles through the headphones and she sits bolt upright. Something is there!"

Yancey goes on to say, "For long stretches, achingly long stretches, I have also sat with my headphones on, desperate for some message from the other world, yearning for reassuring contact, and heard only static."

Notwithstanding the length of time a believer has participated in The Relay, the safe assumption is that Yancey's suggestion of hearing only static for "achingly long stretches" will resonate. A similarly safe assumption would be: If any of the Bible's 66 Books had the potential to break through the static or silence you might be experiencing, the five penned by John come to mind.

Although we don't yet have the luxury of seeing The Redeemer face-to-face as John did (at least not yet), his accounts do give us a glimpse into what the world may have looked like seen through the eyes of Christ. By leaning up against Jesus' breast, John had the rare angle of looking outward while Christ spoke. This likely explains his uncanny way of presenting his material that reverberates across a widely varied audience. His relatability, his distinctive notes, how he innately pinpoints and speaks to the neediest human emotion at the exact right time, are all unique to John. His themes like care, compassion and understanding, emanate from The Savior's reassuring voice.

> *"To him the doorkeeper opens, and the sheep hear His voice, and He calls His own sheep by name and leads them out. When He puts forth all His own, He goes ahead of them, and the sheep follow Him because they know His voice. A stranger they simply will not follow, but will flee from him, because they do not know the voice of strangers."* (John 10:3-5)

There's a tender story about a farmer, his litter of puppies and a little boy that illustrates this ingrained longing to be known:

A farmer had some puppies he needed to sell. He painted a sign advertising the pups and set about nailing it to a post on the edge of his yard. As he was driving the last nail into the post, he felt a tug on his overalls. He looked down into the eyes of a little boy. "Mister," he said, "I want to buy one of your puppies." "Well," said the farmer, as he rubbed the sweat off the back of his neck, "these puppies come from fine parents and cost a good deal of money." The boy dropped his head for a moment. Then reaching deep into his pocket, he pulled out a handful of change and held it up to the farmer. "I've got thirty-nine cents. Is that enough to take a look?"

"Sure," said the farmer. And with that, he let out a whistle, "Here, Dolly!" he called. Out from the doghouse and down the ramp ran Dolly followed by four little balls of fur. The little boy pressed his face against the chain link fence. Slowly another little ball appeared; this one noticeably smaller. Down the ramp it slid. Then in a somewhat awkward manner the little pup began hobbling toward the others, doing its best to catch up. "I want that one," the little boy said, pointing to the runt. The farmer knelt down at the boy's side and said, "Son, you don't want that puppy. He will never be able to run and play with you like these other dogs would." With that, the little boy stepped back from the fence, reached down and began rolling up one leg of his trousers. In doing so, he revealed a steel brace running down both sides of his leg attaching itself to a specially made shoe. Looking back up at the farmer, he said, "You see sir, I don't run too well myself and he will need someone who understands."

We all yearn to feel understood, to be known fully, and John's writings have a knack for doing just that.

> "Sometimes the strength within you is not a big fiery flame for all to see, it is just a tiny spark that whispers softly, 'You got this, keep going!'" —Unknown

A kind word or a gentle whisper of assurance, whether spoken by Jesus, John, a friend whom we most trust, or for that matter a complete stranger, all have the remarkable ability to instill confidence in the least of us, bolstering us to stay in the race *"so that when He appears, we may have confidence and not shrink away from Him in shame at His coming."* (1 John 2:28)

This is the Way, Walk in It

"Momma always says there's an awful lot you could tell about a person by their shoes. Where they're going. Where they've been . . . I've worn lots of shoes. I bet if I think about it real hard, I could remember my first pair of shoes . . . Momma said they'd take me anywhere." —Forrest Gump

That's how the opening scene of the blockbuster movie *Forrest Gump* began, with the simple man from Greenbow, Alabama, sitting on a park bench in Savannah, Georgia.

The Apostle John, similarly ostracized as a simple man in his day, and his shoes (actually sandals) could tell us a lot about the ground he covered over the course of 90 years. Beginning with the original call on his life while mending nets along the Sea of Galilee: *"follow Me . . . from now on you will be catching men,"* (Luke 5:10) or the time he traversed a high mountain to hear God say of His Son "This is My beloved Son, listen to Him!" (Mark 9:7), or even the day he stood atop a blood-drenched hill called Golgotha, helplessly watching his beloved Savior die, all the way until his exile on the island prison of Patmos, only to finish out his days being carried about on a stretcher according to reliable tradition.

John's early steps were not without setbacks, causing him to live up to the fiery "son of thunder" surname bestowed upon him by Jesus. He called for fire to be rained down from Heaven to annihilate an entire Samaritan village for being inhospitable (Luke 9:54), and he rebuked an outsider for casting out demons because he was not among the elite inner-circle of the Twelve Disciples. (Luke 9:49) John MacArthur's assessment was equally unflattering: "It is clear from the Gospel accounts that John was capable of behaving in the most sectarian, narrow-minded, unbending, reckless and impetuous fashion. He was volatile. He was brash. He was aggressive."

John was never one to stay down, however, or, as Abraham Lincoln suggested: "I am not concerned that you have fallen—I am concerned that you arise."

In his life as well as yours, there comes an immensely defining moment where the past is left there in the past, allowing you to progress forward *"so that your joy may be made full."* (2 John 1:12) There is freedom in that place and John basked in it. The Good News demands you bask there as well. *"If we confess our sins, He is faithful and righteous to forgive us our sins and to cleanse us from all unrighteousness."* (1st John 1:9)

Allow me here to share some practical advice: Absolutely nothing stalls one's relay more than unforgiveness, especially a refusal to forgive oneself. It is not feasible to pass the Gospel like a baton to another without first receiving it yourself.

After all, John was compelled to say, *"This is how we know that we belong to the Truth and how we set our hearts at rest in His presence: If our hearts condemn us, we know that God is greater than our hearts, and he knows everything. Dear friends, if our hearts do not condemn us, we have confidence before God."* (1st John 3:19-21)

As a participant in The Relay, your walk or run will never progress as God intends until you see yourself through the lens in which your Heavenly Father sees you: uncondemned! Failure to view yourself as such is unbiblical at best and debilitating at worst.

If you will stop long enough to notice the subtle yet significant way John perceives himself through the lens of his Friend Jesus, it will minister to you beyond measure: "the one whom Jesus loved." Allow that to sink in. John was able to lay aside his former "son of thunder" identity so that "the one whom Jesus loved" might press on.

If God sees you for who you are in Christ, not for who you were without Him, why would you do differently? A lot of truth can be found in another Forrest Gump quote: "Momma always said you got to put the past behind you before you can move on." It's possible that the writer was inspired by Isaiah 43:18: "Do not call to mind the former things, Or ponder things of the past."

Practically speaking, the next time satan reminds you of your past, you remind him of his future.

"Most people never run far enough on their first wind to find out they've got a second." —William James

Another compelling encouragement for us is to not only see John get back up and regroup, but to witness his second wind kick into full force as he closes out his Gospel. Not only was he the sole male friend to console Jesus as He hung on the cross but was also given the task that is one of the most sacred responsibilities ever given to man: caring for Jesus' soon-to-be childless mother, Mary. Furthermore, during first light on Easter Sunday, it was John who "ran ahead faster than Peter and came to the tomb first," becoming the first ever to genuinely "see and believe" unto salvation. It's as if one runner wrote to cheer on other runners to stay in the race: "The race is not always to the swift, but to those who keep on running."

In order for the ever-expanding Relay to outlive the first century, John and the other Apostles had the foresight to leave something tangible behind: the 27 Books that make up our New Testament. Had John merely journaled his interactions with Christ for his own personal use, he would have placed a period after "concerning the Word of Life" at the end of verse one rather than continuing with verse two as you can see below:

[1]"What was from the beginning, what we have heard, what we have seen with our eyes, what we have looked at and touched with our hands, concerning the Word of Life— [2]and the life was manifested, and we have seen and testify and proclaim to you the eternal

life which was with the Father and was manifested to us— ³what we have seen and heard we proclaim to you also, so that you too may have fellowship with us; and indeed our fellowship is with the Father, and with His Son Jesus Christ. ⁴These things we write, so that our joy may be made complete." (1st John 1:1-4)

There is, however, one major stipulation related to the writings—they will only speak to you or break through as much as you are dedicated to reading them. Stated differently, you must tread them frequently. Here's what I mean.

The Hebrew word *daresh* is used in Scripture and means "to frequent" a place or "tread there often." Let's say, for instance, you were to come across a worn path or trail in a forest; it would be obvious someone or something had frequented there *(daresh)* before you arrived. The Bible uses that same word to describe what occurs when someone seeks God and studies His word. *"Seek the LORD while He may be found"* would more correctly be read *"Frequent the Lord and tread before Him often while He may be found."* (Isaiah 55:6)

To frequent or tread often in The Presence of the Lord will not go unnoticed by Him nor the outside world: *"Now as they observed the confidence of Peter and John and understood that they were uneducated and untrained men, they were amazed, and began to recognize them as having been with Jesus."* (Acts 4:13)

You must likewise live in such a way that others may recognize that you have been with Jesus. As you dedicate ample time to open up and read John's letters to you, see if you can pinpoint a favorite tendency of his: coupling of series of opposites, such as light and darkness, Heaven and Earth, first and last, which was a common rhetorical device authors used in antiquity to express how all-encompassing something was. Like in Revelation 21:6 when Jesus declared, *"I am the Alpha and the Omega, the beginning and the end."*

To borrow that same writing habit of John's and apply it back to him, if ever a runner lived, who from A to Z, start to finish, beginning to end, first to last, strived above all to pass off the Word of God like a baton, it was, without a doubt, John. When poring over his manuscripts, it's as if he is screaming out, "if you don't get anything else from my letters get this: You must get Jesus, you must get His word." And it's impossible to get One without the other because even *"His name is called The Word of God."* (Revelation 19:13)

Consider the following examples. As John deliberated over his portrayal of Christ in the Holy Script that bore his name, he had to pick a starting point. Under the inspiration of the Holy Spirit, quill in one hand, parchment in the other, what motif might he choose for his first verse? *"In the beginning was the Word, the Word was with God, the Word was God."* (John 1:1) That's not all. Any guesses as to what motif he selected to conclude his very last verse? The Word, as 'Biblios' just so happens to be the final word in the Greek text of his Gospel! (John 21:25)

John expressly closed out his Gospel in the same manner in which he opened it—it's all about the Word.

The pattern remains constant throughout, as illustrated in the Book of Revelation. Its opening introduction begins with John testifying "to the Word of God," and for its salutation you can see for yourself: *"I testify to everyone who hears the words of the prophecy of this book (Biblios): if anyone adds to them, God will add to him the plagues which are written in this book (Biblios); and if anyone takes away from the words of the book (Biblios) of this prophecy, God will take away his part from the tree of life and from the holy city, which are written in this book (Biblios)."* (Revelation 22:18-19)

After six decades of charging after Christ and entreating others to do the same, John's single-minded mission of transporting God's Law never waned. Spurgeon's observation of Scripture's effects seems especially fitting for John: "Nobody ever outgrows Scripture; the book widens and deepens with our years." This means the Bible is like a river cutting through hard rock as erosion sets in . . . it gets wider and deeper as time goes on. Over the years as the word flows it continually erodes the hardness of our hearts. It causes us to grow wider and deeper than ever before.

That's why John's letters are so universally adored—of the 40-plus authors in Scripture no one directs and redirects the reader more to Christ and His word than John does. This makes the case that John the Apostle of Love could likewise be called John the Apostle of the Word.

The master blues musician Jimmy Reed was a sharecropper's son from the Mississippi Delta. If you listen to his records, you'll hear something curious: a woman's voice very faint in the background. Legend has it that Jimmy was so absorbed in the music that he couldn't remember the words to his own songs. His devoted wife would coach him through his recording sessions by whispering the lyrics in his ear.

In the same way, resolve to immerse yourself in John's literature. Listen for the faint murmurs as well—those melodic, prodding whispers of the Holy Spirit that directed each stroke of his pen, convincing you that they were written with just you in mind. Although the melodies or tunes might differ, one distinguishing characteristic will always remain the same: You must get Jesus. You must get His word.

"If I should say, 'My foot has slipped,' Your lovingkindness, O LORD, will hold me up." (Psalm 94:18)

Insomuch as you may have allowed the static of your all-too busy life to drown the Messiah's whispers out, or have recently strayed to the right or left due to a prior indiscretion, rest assured: After you repent, those once-distinct murmurs still exist and are available this very instant. You must, however, be still and be quiet and intently listen for them. Notice the emphasis on listen, not hear, in that a profound chasm exists between the two. As you read this, a degree of background noise can be heard that, up to this point, has gone largely unnoticed. You heard it all along, but until now, you really weren't listening to it. This concept also applies to Scripture. If you are not careful, it could grievously be relegated to background noise . . . and that is not what God intended. Not at all.

Once the Lord of Creation has your attention and you listen intently to decipher what it is He has to say to you, it's imperative you follow His lead accordingly. "He, your Teacher will no longer hide Himself, but your eyes will behold your Teacher. Your ears will hear a word behind you, 'This is the way, walk in it,' whenever you turn to the right or to the left." (Isaiah 30:20-21)

A.W. Tozer described the process this way: "The progression will be something like this: First a sound as of a Presence walking in the garden. Then a voice, more intelligible, but still far from clear. Then the happy moment when the Spirit begins to illuminate the Scriptures and that which had been only a sound, or, at best, a voice, now becomes an intelligible word, warm and intimate and clear as the word of a dear friend. Then will come light and life and best of all, ability to see and rest in and embrace Jesus Christ as Savior and Lord of all."

"My sheep listen to my voice; I know them, and they follow me."
(John 10:27, NIV)

The Relay as it pertains to John adorably played itself out in the life of my family many years ago, you could say through a sequence of whispers, originating with Jesus The Great Shepherd of the sheep, then to John His under-shepherd, then to me the shepherd of my family, then on to a little lamb—my precious daughter Bailey. Let me explain.

When Bailey was 4 years old, she was sick with a stomach bug, and I barely made it home in time to tuck her in. Although she didn't feel well, I assumed she felt that getting away from our nightly routine would only make her feel worse, leading her to ask for a bedtime story. I happily obliged, and as The Lord would have it, I had the perfect story from a sermon I'd been preparing earlier in the day. The text for Sunday's message came from 1st John 3:16-19:

"We know love by this, that He laid down His life for us; and we ought to lay down our lives for the brethren. But whoever has the world's goods, and sees his brother in need and closes his heart against him, how does the love of God abide in him? Little children, let us not love with word or with tongue, but in deed and truth."

Kneeling beside her bed, I began in a soft voice:

A little boy had a very rare blood disorder, and the only way he could survive would be to find another person with his exact blood type who would be willing to undergo a blood transfusion. (Of course, I brought this down to a level a child could relate to, and as you'll see shortly Bailey's childlike understanding entailed far greater faith than my own). After an extensive search, the doctors weren't able to identify the right candidate and time was quickly running out. As a last result, one of the physicians made the uncomfortable suggestion they test the boy's younger sister to see if she might qualify as a donor. The procedure would be risky and endanger her life, but there were simply no remaining options. After running a series of tests, it was determined she was in fact a perfect match. Unsure how to proceed, the parents decided to share all the details with their daughter and allow her to make the final decision. As it turned out, she agreed.

The following day they went through with the transfusion, and happy to say it was a complete success. When the head physician went back to recovery to check on the girl and congratulate her for saving her brother's life, he was taken aback to find her crying. When asked why, her only reply was, "when do I die?" her lip quivering. Unsure what she meant, the doctor repeated his question, "Why are you so upset?" Her reply was the same, and that's when the realization sunk in: All along she thought that giving her blood to let her brother live meant that she had to die. And yet she did it anyway.

I went on to tie that little girl's brave deed of sacrificial love back into what Jesus did on the cross, explaining how we were sick and how He had to take our sickness so that we could be healed. That's when the top Daddy-Daughter connection took place between the two of us over the course of our 21-year relationship, which I can only describe like this: We were locked in—locked into the moment, locked into each other, the Holy Spirit; we simply were and it was no less real than the densest matter. I was overly emotional, why, exactly, I still do not know—perhaps I had overly complicated the sheer simplicity of the Gospel Message for far too long, shame on me for placing theological astuteness above childlike wonderment. Whatever the reason, what I do know is: I can still see her pursed lips, her slight grin, her wholehearted belief in what I said next: "Bailey, do you know I love you so much I would be willing to die for you? Do you believe that?"

Unquestionably she did, her eyes said as much. "Yes Daddy."

"Bailey, do you know Jesus loved you so much He did die for you? Do you believe that?"

Her reply was the same, and I promise she 100% meant it—I'm certain of it because her eyes said as much. I led us in a short prayer and must confess I didn't expect The Great Physician to answer it. "Dear Lord, if it be Your will, please let me be sick instead of Bailey so she could feel better. Amen." Later, I didn't recall much about that mini-sermon preached at my daughter's bedside; evidently, she did.

A few months later, I became ill with the flu and was quarantined to my bedroom, a necessary precaution taken in the days preceding Tamiflu's release. Bailey kept insisting to her mother she had to thank me for something; it would make me feel better, she promised. Jill eventually relented, as did I, a gesture more for Bailey's sake than mine considering how horrible I felt. We allowed her to stand just inside the door of our bedroom but no closer. "Daddy, Jesus answered your prayers, so thank you." The furthest thing on my mind was gratefulness or answered prayers, or anything else for that matter except for survival . . . but it did make me curious.

"Okay, Bailey, that is so sweet of you to say, but thank you for what?"

Hardly able to contain her excitement, she continued, "Jesus answered your prayers, and that's why you're sick, not me. Thank you, Daddy."

A father's bedside prayer to drive home a theological truth to his little girl is one thing. A little girl's sincere willingness to die so that her brother might live is wholly another. The Lamb of God who *"came that they may have life, and have it abundantly,"* and *"laid down His life for the sheep,"* (John 10:10-11) well that's entirely another, and the most Divine act of all. *"Greater love has no one than this, that one lay down his life for his friends."* (John 15:13)

In closing, play your respective role in the furtherance of The Relay by becoming the channel through whom those whispers continue to be heard by lost sheep in desperate need of a Shepherd—or in Yancey's line, those "desperate for some message from the other world, yearning for reassuring contact." Correspondingly, pray that the whispers will be received as the Lord sees fit, even if He answers in the manner you least expect (as in the case with my daughter). Jesus does take great delight in the asking.

> *"This is the confidence which we have before Him, that, if we ask anything according to His will, He hears us. And if we know that He hears us in whatever we ask, we know that we have the requests which we have asked from Him."* (1st John 5:14-15)

Please pray He might kindly oblige. After all, The Relay has to continue; the race must go on.

8

PETER

On Your Mark, GO! Get Set

"How you start is important, very important, but in the end, it is how you finish that counts. It is easier to be a self-starter than a self-finisher. The victor in the race is not the one who dashes off swiftest but the one who leads at the finish. In the race for success, speed is less important than stamina. The sticker outlasts the sprinter in life's race." —B. C. Forbes

---

Peter, a former fisherman turned evangelist, could best be described as an unorthodox, "runners on your mark, GO! get set" kind of guy, as opposed to the traditional "runners on your mark, get set, go!" type.

When reading the four Gospels, Peter seemed incapable of perfecting the art of blind handoffs. A blind handoff takes place in a relay when the first runner reaches a predetermined spot on the track, signaling to the next runner to take off without looking back. As the second runner gains momentum, he waits to hear the verbal command "stick!" before extending his hand backward to receive the baton. The purpose of a blind handoff is to maximize speed and efficiency.

Peter's habit was to impulsively take off running minus the one thing that mattered most—the baton! The result was always the same—a false start. Forget the pass; he just ran.

"Life doesn't give you all the practice races you need," lamented Jesse Owens, the legendary four-time gold medalist in the 1936 Berlin Games who also made sporting history when he broke five world records and equaled a sixth in the space of 45 minutes.

It's a particularly fitting quote applicable to the Apostle Peter's life, as well. Peter's early career was plagued by a long streak of potential ministry-ending false starts.

"Track and Field's one-false-start rule is simply the cruelest," declared a *Washington Post* article covering the Rio Olympics on August 16, 2016:

> It's been called the cruelest rule in Olympic sports, if not all sports: A runner is disqualified from a track event after just one false start. No warnings, no do-overs. You're done. It happened to French sprinter Wilhem Belocian on Monday night in his 110-meter hurdles preliminary heat. Four years of Olympic training, gone a millisecond too soon.

Thankfully for Peter, the Bible teaches us that our God is a long-suffering God as he attested from firsthand experience: *"The Lord is not slow about His promise as some count slowness, but is patient toward you, not wishing for any to perish but for all to come to repentance."* (2nd Peter 3:9) The Lord is well within His rights to settle accounts over wrongdoings today (like the one-false-start disqualification rule), but by long suffering, He may choose to extend His verdict for another. Only a fool, however, would confuse long suffering with a license to sin. At times, Peter got dangerously close to being that fool.

You might recall the cringeworthy episode when Peter rebuked God's Son for predicting the impending trial and execution He was to face in Jerusalem!

CHAPTER 8

"Peter took Him aside and began to rebuke Him, saying, 'God forbid it, Lord! This shall never happen to You.' But He turned and said to Peter, 'Get behind Me, Satan! You are a stumbling block to Me; for you are not setting your mind on God's interests, but man's.'" (Matthew 16:21-23)

Or the later mortifying assertion made during the Last Supper:

"Then Jesus said to them, 'You will all fall away because of Me this night, for it is written, "I will strike down the Shepherd, and the sheep of the flock shall be scattered." But after I have been raised, I will go ahead of you to Galilee.' But Peter said to Him, 'Even though all may fall away because of You, I will never fall away.' Jesus said to him, 'Truly I say to you that this very night, before a rooster crows, you will deny Me three times.' Peter said to Him, 'Even if I have to die with You, I will not deny You.'" (Matthew 26:31-35)

Western novelist Stephen Bly says that in the days of America's Old West, there were two types of friends: runners and standers. At the first sign of trouble, the runner would bolt—abandoning you to whatever peril you were facing. But a stander would stick with you no matter the circumstances. Unfortunately, you wouldn't know which kind of friend you had until trouble came. And then it was too late—unless your friend was a stander.

—"Be a Stander," OurDailyBread.com

Regrettably, Peter promised to be a stander but proved to be a runner, at least initially, buckling under pressure by denying any association with Christ, going so far as refusing to even utter his Friend by name. Peter *"began to curse and swear, 'I do not know this man you are talking about!' Immediately a rooster crowed a second time. And Peter remembered how Jesus had made the remark to him, 'Before a rooster crows twice, you will deny Me three times.' And he began to weep."* (Mark 14:71-72)

Under normal circumstances and under the heavy burden of such lapses, most individuals would either give up and walk away, or grow timid and play it safe. Not so with Peter. As far as giving up was concerned, the culture of the day did not allow quitting under any circumstances; even athletic events outlawed competitors from withdrawing no matter the degree of difficulty encountered, unexpected or otherwise. More important, Peter recalled what His Master had said, *"No one, after putting his hand to the plow and looking back, is fit for the kingdom of God."* (Luke 9:62) Yes, he had fallen, but he had also put his hand to the plow (much like putting one's hand to the baton). To let go or to turn back was never an option.

As far as Peter becoming timid or playing it safe going forward . . . not a chance! No chance, even though a real threat of mental hurdles would have been warranted, as any competitive runner could attest who's struggled with false starts. Christ the Cornerstone had previously enlisted Peter the rock to build His church, such that the Gates of Hades would not prevail against it. *"I also say to you that you are Peter, and upon this rock I will build My church; and the gates of Hades will not overpower it!"* (Matthew 16:18)

The Relay was not to be thwarted nor the race to be stopped; in fact, Peter would be the one to emerge from the pack and lead the fray as first among his equals. Again, to cite C. S. Lewis: "You can't go back and change the beginning. But you can start where you are and change the ending."

True to form, Peter was quick to make fresh starts to change the ending, two key instances of which are below, both stemming from risk-taking: the time Peter stepped out of the boat, and the first time he took his stand. Let's look at each in that order.

Risk #1: Stepping Out of the Boat

"The most striking thing about highly effective leaders is how little they have in common. What one swears by, another warns against. But one trait stands out: Effective leaders are willing to take risks."
—Larry Osbourne

In his book *Reaching for the Invisible* God, Philip Yancey shares the following about risks:

> In a famous allegorical dilemma, a 14th century monk told of a donkey who confronts two equally attractive, equally distant bales of hay. The animal stares, hesitates, stares some more and eventually perishes because he has no logical justification for moving toward one bale or the other.
>
> Without an element of risk, there is no faith. Like the donkey torn between two bales, this middle ground may represent the greatest danger. Faith means striking out, with no clear end in sight and perhaps even no clear view of the next step. It means following, trusting, holding out a hand to an Invisible Guide.

Of all the things that can be said of Peter and his impulsivity, we can't say he was likely to perish from hesitation; rather, he was willing to take risks demonstrated in the story below:

> *"[24]But the boat was already a long distance from the land, battered by the waves; for the wind was contrary. [25]And in the fourth watch of the night He came to them, walking on the sea. [26]When the disciples saw Him walking on the sea, they were terrified, and said, 'It is a ghost!' And they cried out in fear. [27]But immediately Jesus spoke*

to them, saying, 'Take courage, it is I; do not be afraid.'

"²⁸Peter said to Him, 'Lord, if it is You, command me to come to You on the water.' ²⁹And He said, 'Come!' And Peter got out of the boat and walked on the water and came toward Jesus. ³⁰But seeing the wind, he became frightened, and beginning to sink, he cried out, 'Lord, save me!' ³¹Immediately Jesus stretched out His hand and took hold of him, and said to him, 'You of little faith, why did you doubt?'" (Matthew 14:24-31)

Peter, a seasoned fisherman in his own right, along with eleven others, launched an unsuccessful campaign against an unrelenting gale that pounded their vessel as they sailed the Sea of Galilee. It's interesting to note by their own strength, in their own power and through their own efforts, no headway was made after nine exhausting hours. Again, these were experienced seamen making zero progress by their own abilities—a timeless spiritual principle applicable to all. As is often the case, Jesus shows up at the apex of desperation. Jesus is fond of our desperation, very much so it seems, perfectly timing His *"take courage, it is I: do not be afraid"* right on the heels of our terrified *"cry out in fear;"* His voice somehow rising up and transcending over the storm that rages when we need to hear it most.

Never one to oscillate, Peter took a risk by stepping up and stepping out onto the water. After some initial success, he fell flat before his Christ and before his fellow sailors, humbled, to say the least. There's no shortage of storylines here, including an all-too-predictable assortment emanating from the majority of pulpits, basically telling the rest of us, *"Don't be like Peter!"* Peter is chided for not having enough faith; Christ rebuked him for his lack of it. We're reminded to keep our eyes fixed on Jesus rather than on the waves and torrents of worry that cause us to sink. While those statements are true, there are times when the only step worse than a misstep is no step at all. And this was one of those times.

Out of a twelve-man crew, only one trusted Jesus to the point of acting on it: *"And Peter got out of the boat and walked on the water."* As a result, in the history of humankind, only one person has actually walked on top of the sea. What might it have felt like as his first sandal touched down on the water that evening? Could he feel the waves surging beneath his toes or did the water still beneath his feet? No disciple but Peter could ever know the answers to those questions. Olympian Eric Liddell was right to say, "You will know as much of God, and only as much of God, as you are willing to put into practice."

This is a good stopping point to share several practical suggestions. If prior false starts are hindering you from acting on whatever you're feeling led to do, please know the Gospel does allow you to hit reset. That means, in respect to *"your former manner of life,"* (Ephesians 4:22-24) leave it behind. It's of no use now. One's race of a lifetime cannot be defined by any one stride. The clock's been reset. It sure seems like a nice day to go for a run.

The playwright Alan Bennett observed, "Sometimes there is no next time, no time-outs, no second chances. Sometimes it's now or never." So regroup and get a move on!

To say the Kingdom of God desperately needs you is no exaggeration. As you'll see, Peter regrouped and got back in the race, and the Lord used him greatly because of it. The last thing the Church needs at this critical juncture is for believers to play it safe when it comes to transporting the baton, evangelizing and sharing the faith, despite how intimidating or embarrassing that may seem. If by telling others that Jesus has risen is risky, then please take those risks.

"The greater danger for most of us lies not in setting our aim too high and falling short; but in setting our aim too low and achieving our mark." —Michelangelo

In his book *The True Measure of a Man,* author Richard Simmons shares the following:

> The fear of failure also causes individuals to play it safe in life. We find ourselves avoiding reasonable risks that we should probably take. Not wanting to look bad in the eyes of others, our judgment becomes critically impaired, and we find ourselves not pursuing viable opportunities—even when failure is a remote possibility. Tony Campolo tells of a study done a number of years ago by a group of sociologists. They interviewed a large number of people, and the only criteria to be chosen for the study was that you had to be at least ninety-five years old. They were asked this one question: If you could live your life over again, what would you do differently? One of the most common answers of this group of elderly people was, "If I could go back and live my life over again, I would have taken more risks." What strikes me with this answer is that these people in their twilight years realized what a mistake it was to play it safe over the course of their lives because they were afraid to fail. If you think about it, most of the great accomplishments in life are the result of people willing to step out of their comfort zones into the unknown, knowing that failure is a possibility.

Peter never lived to see the twilight years. If dying of old age meant denying Christ, he would have none of it. Beginning on the Day of Pentecost and continuing to his martyrdom, he had staked his rock-solid commitment to preaching the Gospel, never again to buckle under pressure.

According to reliable tradition, he implored his executioners to crucify him "not in the usual way, but head downwards, in order, said he, that the servant be not seen in the

position once taken by the Master. His request was granted."
(Regina Magazine)

Pastor and author David Platt said it best: "Radical obedience to Christ is not easy . . . It's not comfort, not health, not wealth, and not prosperity in this world. Radical obedience to Christ risks losing all these things. But in the end, such risk finds its reward in Christ. And he is more than enough for us."

Risk #2: Taking His Stand

3:00 PM Friday, 30AD

Thousands upon thousands of Middle Easterners had the privilege of seeing, hearing, even feeling the skin of God—as hard as that is to fathom, all without filter . . . the renowned Galilean named Jesus.

As I read the Gospel record, I try to overhear behind the written text the steady volley of bold assertions by His would-be adherents—vowing to carry crosses at The Nazarene's first bidding, follow Him at all costs, even die as His martyrs in hopes of changing the world as they knew it.

At 3:00 PM that Good Friday, 30 AD, how sorrowed The King of Kings must have felt as He scanned the battlefield of Golgotha, ominously nicknamed "The Place of the Skull," saddened at how devoid it was of all those would-be followers. All but a few handfuls among those tens of thousands remained: "At the first sign of trouble, the runner would bolt—abandoning you to whatever peril you were facing."

Thirty-nine hours later as the risen Jesus stood opposite a supposedly immovable stone, the number of devotees had seemingly dwindled further down to one: Mary Magdalene. She was the first to risk her entirety for the Savior (thus proving herself to be a stander, not a runner; "a stander would stick with you no matter the circumstances.") She was also the first relayer in history to convey she had seen the Resurrected Christ: *"Mary Magdalene came, announcing to the disciples, 'I have seen the Lord.'"* (John 20:18) Hers was the initial testimony used to kickstart The Relay into high gear; that's when the groundswell really began.

News that Jesus was alive traveled quickly. The newly formed faith grew exponentially from one to three, then 11, 12, settling at 120 within a matter of days. Jesus had prophesied explosive growth was at hand: *"You will receive power when the Holy Spirit has come upon you; and you shall be My witnesses both in Jerusalem, and in all Judea and Samaria, and even to the remotest part of the earth."* (Acts 1:8)

The seismic upsurge of Christianity in the days to come could not be overstated. It was like an earthquake—Jerusalem at the epicenter; primary and secondary shockwaves spreading throughout Judea and Samaria; tremors felt at Earth's remotest parts.

To prevent the Disciples from embarking once again by their own strength, in their own power and through their own efforts, only to find themselves in the same predicament as The Sea of Galilee, Jesus left strict orders: *"Gathering them together, He commanded them not to leave Jerusalem, but to wait for what the Father had promised, 'Which,' He said, 'you heard of from Me; for John baptized with water, but you will be baptized with the Holy Spirit not many days from now.'"* (Acts 1:4-5)

Peter was never one to wait, especially having seen Christ alive and desirous to tell the known world as much (surely no less painstaking than freezing after "runners on your mark, get set . . . "). It did seem he had learned a lesson by remaining still for the moment; otherwise, his labor would have fallen flat on its face right out of the gate.

"Oh give me that Book! At any price, give me the Book of God! I have it: here is knowledge enough for me. Let me be 'a man of one Book.'"

— Methodism founder John Wesley

Once the curtain opens in the Book of Acts, the reader is able to peer into The Upper Room where the 120 were congregating. After a likely volley of awkward glances and exchanges among those present, each waiting to see who might take a risk by stepping to the fore, their leader finally emerged: *"At this time Peter stood up in the midst of the brethren, and said 'Brethren, the Scripture had to be fulfilled.'"*

Did you catch that? The very first words he spoke came from the Bible: *"Brethren, the Scripture had to be fulfilled."* Peter was coming into his own as a man of one book, having the foresight to advance something far superior to himself— "the prophetic Word made more sure." (2nd Peter 1:19) *"The living and enduring Word of God."* (1st Peter 1:23)

Peter's commitment to Scripture didn't begin and end in Acts Chapter 1. On the Day of Pentecost as recorded in Acts 2, Jesus' promise of Another Helper—The Comforter —came to pass as The Holy Spirit descended from Heaven in a never-before-seen way:

"When the day of Pentecost had come, they were all together in one place. And suddenly there came from heaven a noise like a violent rushing wind, and it filled the whole house where they were sitting. And there appeared to them tongues as of fire distributing themselves, and they rested on each one of them. And they were all filled with the Holy Spirit and began to speak with other tongues, as the Spirit was giving them utterance." (Acts 2:1-4)

As the dust settled, we're told devout men from every nation under Heaven "continued in amazement and great perplexity, saying to one another, *'What does this mean?'"* At which time, Peter proved himself a stander (literally, no longer a runner like at Jesus' trial): *"But Peter, taking his stand with the eleven, raised his voice and declared to them: 'Men of Judea and all you who live in Jerusalem, let this be known to you and give heed to my words . . . "* (Acts 2:14)

The Greek way of saying "taking his stand" is technically "one who holds the ground and does not hesitate or waver, also of one who in the midst of the fight holds his position." While standing his ground, should we be surprised where Peter went next? The Old Testament: *"But this is what was spoken through the prophet Joel . . . "* And he was just getting started.

Peter's Apostleship was marked by a plethora of spreading the Word like none other; the Greek *pletho* means "multiplying," as in Acts 12:24: *"the Word of the Lord continued to grow and to be multiplied (pletho)."*

Study his sermons to see how saturated they are with Old Testament references. Read his epistles and note how they open and close with references to God's Law. The opening of 2nd Peter—*"But know this first of all, that no prophecy of Scripture is a matter of one's own interpretation, for no prophecy was ever made by an act of human will, but men moved by the Holy Spirit spoke from God."* The closing of 2nd Peter: *"This is now, beloved, the second letter I am writing to you in which I am stirring up your sincere mind by way of reminder, that you should remember the words spoken beforehand by the holy prophets and the commandment of the Lord and Savior spoken by your apostles."*

When Peter was commanded *"not to speak or teach at all in the name of Jesus,"* observe his bold reply in Acts 4:19-20, *"Whether it is right in the sight of God to give heed to you rather than to God, you be the judge; for we cannot stop speaking about what we have seen and heard."*

And, most touching of all, the Word seemed to gain a certain sweetness as Peter advanced in age: *"like newborn babies, long for the pure milk of the word, so that by it you may grow in respect to salvation, if you have tasted the kindness of the Lord."* (1st Peter 2:2-3)

Last but not least, even death itself held no sway over the endlessness of God's Statutes: *"the grass withers, and the flower fades, but the Word of the Lord endures forever."* (1st Peter 1:24-25)

It would be easy for you to think, "that's all fine for someone like Saint Peter, but I'm no Peter. In the grand scheme of things, can I really make a lasting difference? Do I really have much to offer?"

Consider the following example:

Sir Michael Costa was a great orchestral conductor in the 19th century. One day he was conducting a rehearsal in which the orchestra was joined by a great chorus. About halfway through the session, with trumpets blaring, drums rolling, and violins singing their rich melody, the piccolo player muttered to himself, "What good am I doing? I might just as well not be playing. Nobody can hear me anyway." So, he kept the instrument to his mouth, but he made no sound. Within moments, the conductor cried, "Stop! Stop! Where's the piccolo?" It was missed by the ear of the most important person of all.

—Richard DeHaan, Our Daily Bread

The God of Creation so structured His church, we might say His symphony, by using individual members to make up the whole. The New Testament analogy from 1st Corinthians 12:12 is that of a body: *"Just as a body, though one, has many parts, but all its many parts form one body, so it is with Christ. Even so, the Body is not made up of one part but of many."*

Be comforted that God handcrafted you with unique gift-edness to build up, or "edify" the Body of Christ. The Greek word for edify is *symphero* from which we get symphony.

The point is, **you have a lane to run** in within the King's grand arena. You have your lane, and you have your race—not Peter's, or anyone else's, for that matter—and your brothers and sisters in Christ are depending on you to run in it to the best of your ability.

Peter was quick to reiterate as much: *"God has given each of you a gift from His great variety of spiritual gifts. Use them well to serve one another."* (1st Peter 4:10, NLT)

To wrap up this chapter, I'd like to call you to action in two ways: "Stand firm!" and "Get up and run!"

Stand Firm!

The idea of standing firm might seem contrary in a book whose theme is running. Nonetheless, as Ecclesiastes reminds us, *"There is an appointed time for everything. And there is a time for every event under Heaven . . . He has made everything appropriate in its time."*

Peter was a runner but he was also a stander, and with grace and time he learned to discern between the two, which made all the difference. That's why he concluded his first Epistle with dual commands to "stand firm!" In 1st Peter 5:8-9 (NLT) he said: *"Stay alert! Watch out for your great enemy, the devil. He prowls around like a roaring lion, looking for someone to devour. Stand firm against him and be strong in your faith. Remember that your family of believers all over the world is going through the same kind of suffering you are."*

In the face of the devil, we must not flee but *"Stand firm!"* which is "to forcefully declare one's personal conviction where they unswervingly stand." The only time a Christian is told to flee, which is *fugitive* in Greek, is in the face of sin, not the devil. In fact, the devil is said to take flight when we stand firm: *"Resist the devil and he will flee from you."* (James 4:7)

In 1st Peter 5:12 (NLT) we're called upon once again to stand firm: "My purpose in writing is to encourage you and assure you that what you are experiencing is truly part of God's grace for you. Stand firm in this grace!"

In an age where runners grossly outnumber standers when it comes to firmly upholding and adhering to the infallible, inerrant Word of God, it would be nice to find your name included in the ranks of the latter. "Courage is contagious," said evangelist Billy Graham, "When a brave man [woman] takes a stand, the spines of others are often stiffened." You be that brave man or woman!

"Get up and Run!"

Olympic runner Eric Liddell is one such man of bravery. He viewed his running as an act of worship. You may know his story; it was celebrated in the 1981 movie *Chariots of Fire.* In his sermon "Strong to the Finish," Craig Brian Larson, coauthor of *Preaching that Connects* and pastor of Lakeshore Assembly of God in Chicago, spoke Liddell's courage:

> Many of you saw the movie *Chariots of Fire.* It was the true story of Eric Liddell, a man who ran for Scotland, then went on to become a missionary. You may recall that he refused to run on the Sabbath, forfeiting some of the awards he probably would have won in the 1924 Olympics.
>
> Well, there was another scene in that movie that may have appeared like Hollywood fiction, but it was also true. One year before the pivotal event in the movie,

Eric Liddell ran in a meet between England, Ireland and Scotland. He ran the 100-, 220- and 440-yard events. In the 440, he got off to a bad start. When that gun sounded, there was a lot of shoving to get in front to the inside lane, the advantageous position. Liddell tangled feet with J. J. Gillies of England and tumbled to the track. He sat there dazed for a moment, not knowing whether he could get up, when the official screamed, "Get up and run!" He jumped to his feet and took off after the pack, which was now a full twenty yards ahead of him. In a quarter mile, that's a big distance to try to make up. In his unorthodox style of running, he took off after the pack. He pulled into fourth place ten yards behind the leader, J. J. Gillies. With forty yards to go, he pulled into third place, then second. Right at the tape, he passed Gillies, stuck his chest out, won the race and collapsed to the track in total exhaustion. Medical personnel had to assist him off the track that day. An article appearing the next day in *The Scotsman* newspaper said, "The circumstances in which Liddell won the race made it a performance bordering on the miraculous. Veterans whose memories take them back thirty-five years and, in some cases, longer in the history of athletics were unanimous in the opinion that Liddell's win in the quarter mile was the greatest track performance they had ever seen."

There's something glorious about getting up off the track after you've been knocked down and running again. Win or lose, you didn't stay down.

Some of you have been knocked down. Maybe Satan has tripped you up. Perhaps you have made some foolish decisions. Perhaps other people have done you wrong.

When we're down on the track, we're embarrassed. We're ashamed. At times we feel self-pity. We're depressed. At times like this, we just feel like staying on the track. But the only real shame is to stay down on the track.

God's word to you is, "Get up and run!" Forget those who have wronged you. Forget what lies behind and run for the prize of the high calling of God in Christ Jesus. You still have a race ahead of you.

9

PAUL

God's Power Perfected through Our Weakness

"No man who really is a man ever cared for the easy task. There is no enjoy-ment in the game that is easily won. It is that in which you have to strain ev-ery muscle and sinew to achieve victory that provides real joy." —*Eric Liddell*

It seemed like any other ordinary Sunday on July 8, 1741, but it was anything but. The only noticeable difference was that a guest preacher was in town to fill the pulpit of the First Church of Christ in Enfield, Connecticut. Interestingly, he was not even the intended preacher that day but a mere stand-in.

The spiritual condition throughout the 13 Colonies was known to be alarmingly poor; even worse, the spiritual condition of Enfield's population was rumored to be poorer still. Expectations for the worship service were bleak at best. However, this was setting the stage for something extraordinary to happen.

After the minister ascended the pulpit, he introduced his sermon by stating, "Their foot shall slide in due time," as taken from Deuteronomy 32:35. Early on, the congregants were duly warned: "he that walks in slippery places is every moment liable to fall, he cannot foresee one moment whether he shall stand or fall the next." This was a timeless caution against slippery slopes, a hazard of which every Christian—and every runner in The Relay—must be aware and take great pains to avoid.

The sermon continued for 48 minutes. From our modern standpoint, the sermon should have fallen flat on its face as a result of the delivery. The preacher was not a dynamic speaker or gifted orator; quite the opposite. Fearing his listeners might see more of him and less of his Savior, this unassuming pastor would read word for word his entire manuscript—in a monotone voice, without hand gestures or eye contact with his listeners.

Had we been in the pews, I assure you we would have commended the out-of-towner's reverence for the "pure and unadulterated word of God" while simultaneously mocking his boring style. Yet the effect of this guest preacher's sermon was anything but boring. Parishioners began shrieking and shouting, "What must we do to be saved?" Some even fainted under the heavy conviction of sin. The scene became so chaotic that the minister had to finish early by wrapping up with this simple, final appeal: "Therefore let everyone that is out of Christ, now awake and fly from the wrath to come!"

Believe it or not, this was the most famous sermon ever preached in what was soon to become America. You may even know the name of that preacher, Jonathan Edwards, and the title of the sermon, "Sinners in the Hands of an Angry God." Despite the man and his manner, God's power was perfected through weakness.

God's Power is Perfected Through Weakness

What if I told you that one of Christianity's most gifted theologians, whose theology shaped Jonathan Edward's understanding of the Bible more than any other, was also by all accounts viewed as weak? His physical appearance was described by his contemporaries as "unimpressive." His oratory skills were labeled by those who knew him best "contemptible." He held no seminary degree, nor any formal training. Not exactly the stellar resume a church search committee would have in mind for their next pastor. But despite what others might consider hindrances of the man and his manner, we must never forget God's power is perfected through our weakness.

Jesus reiterated that very truth to Paul during a private conversation that took place between the two of them in the Third Heaven. Paul kept this a secret for 14 years, maybe because as some have noted, "silence often knows more of Him than speech." Thankfully, however, Paul broke his silence by providing us the transcript of what Christ said to him: "My grace is sufficient for you, for power is perfected in weakness." Paul reacted to this by asserting: "Most gladly, therefore, I will rather boast about my weaknesses, so that the power of Christ may dwell in me. Therefore, I am well content with weaknesses, with insults, with distresses, with persecutions, with difficulties, for Christ's sake; for when I am weak, then I am strong." (2nd Corinthians 12:9-10)

I personally find no more comforting words in all of Scripture. Once it became evident to Paul that his shortcomings provided a more suitable medium for Jesus' strength to be displayed, it had to be one of the most defining moments of his life. It must have freed him up, taken the pressure off— and it should do the same for us.

You may be wondering, "Why such emphasis at this point on human weakness and human hindrances?" The answer is simply to give you this hope: If the Lord could use men like Jonathan Edwards and the Apostle Paul to advance the Gospel as He did, then He can also use you.

The answer is especially relevant because when it comes to personal evangelism, meaning one individual runner sharing Jesus with another (i.e., passing the baton), there are far too many Christians crowding the bleachers simply spectating and far too few participating on the track, while the arena of Christian influence and impact on culture is emptying at a record-breaking pace.

There are two main categories of hindrances that prevent believers from actively engaging others with the Gospel. The first category would include various "nots" and "ills"—"I'm not knowledgeable enough about the Bible" or "I'm too ill-prepared," or "I'm ill-equipped." The second category would be driven more by fear: "What will people think?" or "I don't want to seem weird."

Whatever their reasons, many are in danger of taking up permanent residence in the stadium seats by simply giving up. Marilyn Vos Savant, the Guinness World Records holder for the highest IQ, put it best: "Being defeated is often a temporary condition. Giving up is what makes it permanent."

Olympic medalist and New York City Marathon winner Shalane Flanagan observed: "All runners are tough. Everyone has to have a little fire in them, that even in tough times can't be turned off."

Allow me to try and light a fire underneath you to get you up and running. I hope to do so under three headings:

1. It's the weak things of this world that confound the wise

2. It's your story of change that so compels others to change

3. It's the power of the message, not the messenger

It's the Weak Things of this World that Confound the Wise

Today's followers of Christ should take comfort perusing the annals of our faith's history, seeing how littered the records are with imperfect men and women through whom God still mightily worked. This principle always remains the same: "God has chosen the foolish things of this world to confound the wise." (1st Corinthians 1:26-27)

If ever Christ's strength shone through human weakness, Olympian Eric Liddell's life comes to mind. In life, the newspapers mocked him: "When he appeared in the heats of the 400m at Paris in 1924 his huge sprawling stride, his head thrown back and his arms clawing the air, moved the Americans and other sophisticated experts to ribald laughter." In death, they continued to mock him: "He is remembered among lovers of athletics as probably the ugliest runner who ever won an Olympic championship." (The Guardian)

And yet in 1981, just 50 years after his death, *Chariots of Fire* celebrated Liddell's life as a Christian runner. The movie features one of the most iconic lines in cinematic history: "I've got a lot of running to do first Jennie. You've got to understand. I believe that God made me for a purpose. For China. But He also made me fast. And when I run, I feel His pleasure." Poetically, the memorial headstone erected in his honor at the University of Edinburgh says nothing about Liddell's weaknesses nor his strengths, but only of what His God did in him: "they shall mount up with wings as eagles; they shall run and not be weary." (Isaiah 40:31)

Another example of God using the "foolish" or "weak" things of this world to confound the wise comes from the preaching of Robert Eaglen. Note that an extensive internet search of Robert Eaglen will yield few results, and what little information might surface about him will be largely unflattering. Yet shockingly, the aftereffects of a sermon he preached more than 160 years ago in London can still be felt in Christendom today.

Among the few handfuls of parishioners Robert Eaglen preached to on that cold Sunday morning December 15, 1850, sat an unconverted visitor named Tirshatha. *Christianity*

Today would later describe him as "history's most widely read preacher apart from the Biblical ones. Today, there is available more material written by him than by any other Christian author, living or dead." Tirshatha had spent the previous five years seeking out London's most venerated pastors preaching from the most venerated pulpits each Sunday to simply hear how his sins could be forgiven, after which he recorded, "They never once told me that."

Out of discouragement, he began seeking lesser-known preachers from even lesser-known pulpits, when he happened upon a small chapel in the midst of a snowstorm. The story as he told it:

I sometimes think I might have been in darkness until now had it not been for the goodness of God in sending a snowstorm on Sunday, while I was going to a certain place of worship. When I could go no further, I turned down a side street and came to a little Primitive Methodist Chapel. In that chapel there may have been a dozen or 15 people. I had heard of the Primitive Methodists, how they sang so loudly that they made people's heads ache, but that did not matter to me. I wanted to know how I might be saved, and if they could tell me that I did not care how much they made my head ache.

The minister did not come that morning; he was snowed up, I suppose. At last, a very thin looking man, a shoemaker or tailor or something of that sort, went up into the pulpit to preach. He was not wise enough to preach anything but Christ. He had not learned enough to run away from his text. He was such a poor simpleton that he was obliged to stick to the simple Gospel. Would that there were more simpletons of that sort! I well remember how very simple he was; yet, poor thing, he was in great earnestness.

His text was, "Look unto me, and be ye saved, all the ends of the Earth." (Isaiah 45:22) Just setting his eyes on me, he said: "Young man, you look very miserable, and you will always be miserable, miserable in life and miserable in death if you don't obey my text. But if you obey now, this moment, you will be saved. Young man, look to Jesus Christ. Look. You have nothing to do but to look and live." I looked until I almost could have looked my eyes away. There and then the cloud was gone, the darkness had rolled away, and that moment I saw the sun, and I could have risen that instant and sung with the most enthusiastic of them, of the precious Blood of Christ and the simple faith which looks alone to Him.

That man, called "history's most widely read preacher," was none other than Charles Haddon Spurgeon. In his biography of Spurgeon, *The Prince of Preachers*, Dan Harmon wrote, "It was said the authorities at the little Chapel were half inclined to cancel the service because of the cold. The worshippers were few. What the world might have missed had that service not taken place!"

What the world might have missed had God not used the "foolish" or "weak" things of this world, like Robert Eaglen and Charles Spurgeon, to confound the wise.

The Apostle Paul, Jonathan Edwards, Eric Liddell and a long litany of gifted, and not so gifted, preachers and lay members alike drive home this Biblical reality: Through the so-called "hindrances" of the man and his manner, God's power is perfected through our weakness.

It's Your Story of Change that so Compels Others to Change

Poet and novelist Ben Okri writes: "The fact of storytelling

hints at a fundamental human unease, hints at human imper-
fection. Where there is perfection there is no story to tell."

New Christians, do not forget: It's the story that so compels—the Christian story, with change at its very core, that's
what intrigues us.

Secular educator and cultural anthropologist Michael
Margolis identified the impact that a changed life, or a
changed story, can make on others. He, however, misunder-
stood the Agent who invented change: "The stories we tell
literally make the world. If you want to change the world,
you need to change your story. This truth applies both to
individuals and institutions."

For a case in point, the next time the Olympics roll around
notice what draws the highest viewership—heartfelt stories
with change at their core; those "overcomer" athletes previously discredited by everyone but themselves for being too
"untrained, ill-prepared or ill-equipped" to compete, only to
emerge later on the world's grandest stage during the "Pa-
rade of Nations."

Paul understood the influence of change, brought about
by Jesus, whom the Scriptures inform us is the "Author and
Finisher" of change, and felt so compelled to recount his
story three different times to three different audiences in the
book of Acts.

Jesus' story + Paul's story of change = one heck of a story

For your "heck of a story" to make an impact on others, you
can't keep holding on to it, no more than you could keep a
baton to yourself in a relay. You must pass it forward. The
word of God, like a baton, was designed for movement. To
follow Christ has never been nor will ever be an individual
event. To follow Christ is not a sprint. To follow Christ is not
a marathon. It is a perpetual relay of passing the faith to others as others passed it to you. As defined by the New Testa-

ment, your story is evidence. Your story is evidence identical to that which is presented before witnesses in a court case, and to withhold your account in the courtroom is no more acceptable than withholding it from nonbelievers.

What if your story, or your testimony, is the key piece of evidence necessary to bring about the acquittal of another who stands trial? It very well could be the case. In 30 AD, the early church experienced explosive growth such that entire towns were converted, causing such an uproar that many feared the world was coming to an end. This originated from the stories told by unseasoned, untrained and ill-prepared newcomers to the Christian faith. "The Word of God kept on spreading; and the number of the disciples continued to increase greatly," (Acts 6:7) "Multitudes of men and women, were constantly added to their number." (Acts 5:14)

Know that not everyone will be ecstatic to see you or overjoyed to hear from you—in other words, expect rejection. As a willing disciple, you don't pass the baton in order to be liked; you do it because it is right. The women and men crowding the front lines of a Holy Spirit-driven movement are, in general, not liked. Eric Liddell stressed that "we are all missionaries. Wherever we go we either bring people nearer to Christ or we repel them from Christ." As a missionary, your "new-creation" story revolving around your newly found Savior will often make you a spectacle to the outside world. But if worldliness is defined as "making sin look normal and Godly living strange," it's good to look strange.

In 1st Corinthians 4:9, Paul said: "God has exhibited us apostles last of all, as men condemned to death; because we have become a spectacle (theatre) to the world, both to angels and to men." It's no coincidence Paul likened his testimony or public display of faith to a "spectacle," which is theatre in Greek. Paul was referring to the Roman Coliseum, which attracted 80,000 spectators to watch the theatre, or gladiator fights, that were unfolding before them. The day's first contests began early morning pitting gladiators against savage beasts. If any survived, the noon-time slate forced them to face fierce and well-armed combatants. To escape that sequence of fighting was only a momentary postponement of death. The theater's third and final performance in the afternoon was reserved for those appointed to certain death. They were the ones on exhibit and deemed "last of all." Most astonishing of all would be to witness the Christian willingly entering that same arena "last of all," or voluntarily! No wonder such keen interest was garnered not only from spectators like men and the universe but even the angels who were grossly perplexed: "we have become a spectacle (theatre) to the world, both to angels and to men."

So here's your hope, and it is a very good hope indeed: What if by sharing your story you lost a few friends or were tagged a "spectacle" or "strange"—and yet that served as the agent of change for one unlikely convert. Would it be worth it? Before answering, please keep in mind one additional consideration: Isn't there a story out there somewhere that God used to change you? And yes, it was assuredly worth it then, too.

It's the Power of the Message, not the Messenger

"You Christians look after a document containing enough dynamite to blow all civilization to pieces, turn the world upside down and bring peace to a battle-torn planet. But you treat it as though it is nothing more than a piece of literature." —Gandhi

For argument's sake, let's suppose you still are not convinced that your supposed shortcomings provide a more suitable medium for Jesus' strength to be revealed. One final comfort prevails: If the power emanates from the message alone and not the messenger, then your duty as an intermediary (of the

Gospel) is like the pyrotechnician who lights a stick of dynamite. Once the fuse ignites, he who holds the matches would
be wise to get out of the way.

The Greek word used in the New Testament 120 times for
'power' is *dunamis,* from which we get 'dynamite.' Not once
is the Christian viewed as the dynamite, but the one through
whom the dynamite works. Take, for instance, Romans 1:16
when Paul says: "For I am not ashamed of the Gospel, for it
is the dunamis (power) of God for salvation to everyone who
believes."

This truth can set you free from feelings of inadequacy
when it comes to personal evangelism and embolden you
to unleash the most powerful arsenal on Earth—the Gospel
"which alone is the power unto salvation."

Before closing, I'd like to leave you with a four-fold encouragement that will hopefully alleviate any remaining res-
ervations preventing you from ramping up your personal
evangelistic efforts. First of all, if you are intimidated when
openly talking about Christ to others that's okay; it's actually
an excellent sign and confirms your readiness.

> "I'm always nervous. If I wasn't nervous, it would be
> weird. I get the same feeling at all the big races. It's part
> of the routine, and I accept it. It means I'm there and
> I'm ready."
>
> —Allyson Felix, the only female track and field
> athlete to win six Olympic gold medals

Second, in New Testament times there was no such thing as
a divinity school, or Bible college, or seminary. In fact, there
is not a single recorded use of the word 'seminary' until 1542
AD. The Church depended upon its rank and file members,
not professionals, to grow and expand its borders.

Third, many of the most effective evangelists in the history of Christianity were recent newcomers to the faith with little or no formal training (Billy Graham is an excellent example). The inner zeal of new Christians can't bear to be confined and demands release. It's the mixture of excitement with power and a not so well-packaged spill that makes a newcomer's story so convincing.

Fourth, you just never know who might respond to your message until you start sharing it, actively putting it into practice . . . I sure didn't.

"You will know as much of God, and only as much of God, as you are willing to put into practice."
—Eric Liddell

My wife, Jill, and I were thrilled to move into our first home on LeBron Avenue in Montgomery, Alabama, in 1995. It was a special season of life I'll not soon forget. Life was so good. Christianity was better.

We joined a precious church fellowship, self-described by some members as being "on fire for Jesus." On fire in the good sense, of course, meaning that the Christian excitement taking place inside the church was such that it could not be contained—rather, it continued to spread. If Christianity could be pictured, Eastwood Church was it.

As a newborn follower of Christ, I was perfectly content to learn and observe the teachings and tenets of the faith I'd never heard before. I felt no shame when approaching the Dollar Tree's checkout counter to purchase my very first Bible; I chose an easy-to-understand children's storybook Bible replete with cartoons and illustrations. I did recall how Jesus taught in that same vein—that to enter His Kingdom, childlike faith was required. That seemed like a good enough reason to me for buying a children's Bible.

Shortly thereafter, I began telling every church member who would listen how much truth I was discovering in my storybook Bible. How thrilled I was to be learning so much. How "on fire for Jesus" it made me feel. Identical to Eastwood Church at large, the Christian excitement taking place inside me was such that it could not be contained—it, too, continued to spread. Knowing what I now know, given the chance to take it back at the time, I probably would. But regardless, it was too late; the cat was out of the bag and I would shortly be called upon to act.

If one could picture an ideal stage set for evangelism, this was it. Evidently, the church leadership saw what I didn't, and they called upon me to act upon my growing faith by sharing it with others. The "nots" and "not yets" took root as I resolved to stay comfortably seated in the bleachers. "Maybe later," I reasoned when they floated the suggestion, "but not now. After all, I'm quite happy for the time being to do nothing more than clap and cheer."

Those avoidance tactics failed miserably. Like a momma bird easing her young out of the nest to live on their own, the more seasoned members of the church wasted little time nudging this very reluctant infant in the faith out into the real world. I found myself landing in my own back yard. Enter Dennis Villano.

Dennis was an exterminator living next door. His keen fascination in the world of bugs and how to control them was far greater than my own, but as much as he loved bugs, there was one passion of his that superseded all others, a passion where common ground between us existed: Alabama whitetail deer hunting.

Whenever the subject of whitetails came up, Dennis' entire demeanor would change, and he would ever so predictably and methodically ease into what I referred to as "deep woods mode." He would light up a Marlboro, his thick southern accent thickened and his head cocked downwards; deliberately I suppose, probably to add emphasis once he decided to lift it. Regardless of what was going on around us, Dennis never once broke character, not once. Our topic of conversation was at the moment very serious to him. Toward the end of one such conversation that, true to form, took place with each of us leaning on our respective side of the fence, I casually and with no forethought said I better get back to work to pay the dues on a new hunting club I had just joined an hour south of town. Justifying the cost of the dues to him, and to myself, if truth be told, I stated, "They are steep, yes, but worth every penny in light of the two trophy bucks taken off it last year." And that was that, or so I thought.

A week or so later, we once again found ourselves leaning up against our respective sides of the fence. Ironically, and as only God could orchestrate in this, His Grand Symphony, the structure built for purpose of separating, The Lord overrode by laying common ground. Dennis, just like a bird dog on point awaiting the signal to flush a covey of quail, clearly had something on his mind. It quickly became obvious he had lifted several direct quotes from the hunter's handbook regarding "the ask." The only way I knew was because I'd done the same thing in college; during one hunting season I became so desperate for invitations I committed entire sections of the handbook to memory.

Don't bother trying to locate a hard copy of the hunter's handbook; none exists in printed form. It's an oral tradition shared around fire sources at camp houses throughout the country. It is a clear, concise and universally agreed-upon collection of outdoorsmanship do's and don'ts. For example, if hunter A wanted hunter B to take him hunting, it would be a cardinal sin for A to ask, "Will you take me hunting?" That's far too straightforward and equally desperate, neither of which is appropriate for real hunters. Casual is king when it comes to "the ask." One must converse in a roundabout way, a cool manner, to avoid getting busted.

Dennis' ask played out like this: "You see George, I've got this new 270 rifle and haven't had a chance to shoot it or sight it in. We both know how awful it would be to wound a big buck. Disgusts me to even think. I'd sure like to zero my scope in some time soon. If you ever need a riding buddy for the trip down to your new club, just give me a shout." According to the etiquette of the ask, Dennis' indirect way of asking "will you take me hunting?," was perfectly accept-able—only because it was indirect.

Then it hit me: An entire chapter entitled "Give 'em Heaven" is dedicated to sharing Jesus from a deer stand; the stand in place of the pulpit. I had heard many a man getting saved in the woods; creation directs one's thoughts toward The Creator. Dennis threw out the line. I took the bait. Soon it would be game on.

At the time, I worked in pharmaceutical sales for Merck. On the appointed day, I had put on a luncheon for a group of family practice doctors and was running a few minutes late getting home. As I pulled into my driveway, Dennis was wait-ing, decked out in hunting gear from head to toe. It's hard to imagine how any one human could wear so many articles of camo all at the same time. Somehow, Dennis pulled it off. As I rushed around the house collecting my gear, I noticed some-thing peculiar—a sensation I hadn't felt in years. I was actually jittery, like the butterflies I got public speaking in high school. Because I was in a hurry, I didn't have time to figure out why, just that they were definitely there. I'd find out soon enough.

The farther we drove down the road and the closer we got to the hunting club, the more nervous I became. Since I had vowed to share Jesus before unlocking the club's front gate, my time was running out. Prepped, prayed up and versed up, it was high time to let it flow. And flow it did, flowed south, that is, big time, and did so quickly. My spiel bombed something like this:

> "Dennis, the Bible says we have this problem that makes us sin. I mean, we sin and that's not my problem . . . Maybe it is our problem, I guess. It's somebody's problem. Check that! Anyway, there is a verse in Scripture that says, "all of us are like sheep, because sheep sin . . ." Wait a minute, sheep can't sin. Anyway, Jesus loves me and that's cool. I just thought I should share that . . ." With no sinkhole, tornado or natural disaster nearby to drive into, all I could muster was, "Would you prefer the Honey Hole stand or the one at Rattlesnake Ridge?"

This explains those pre-trip jitters. My prepped, prayed up and versed up "Gospel presentation" was a complete disaster from the get-go. Any other day I would have settled into my stand and pulled out my trusty Topical Memory System cards and started memorizing them, looking up ever so often to see the big one. But not that day. When looking back over my ministry and all the talks and presentations I've given over the years this was the worst by far. I can actually remember that sick feeling in the pit of my stomach of letting myself down, Dennis down, even God down. I was miserable.

My theology—my understanding of Who God is and how He operates—would become forever altered the following morning. Rather than politely knocking at the front door waiting to be invited in, Dennis plowed right into my den in what I thought was a panicked situation. His demeanor had been radically transformed—he actually looked physically different from the day before. An air of "lightness" had replaced the former load of "heaviness," making it difficult to distinguish the shine emanating from him from the day's first light just behind him.

"What's wrong? Is everything okay?" I asked, to which he responded, "I've never been more okay in my entire life."

He went on to explain with uncharacteristic eloquence how something wonderful had happened the night before, how he was now a changed man, how he had given his life to Jesus.

"After you shared your faith with me yesterday," he continued, "I realized for the first time that if I were the only person on Earth, Jesus would have carried that cross just for me. Jesus loved me so much that He died not just for others . . . He died for me."

Those words may be some of the sweetest sounds Earth ever heard; if Heaven could be spoken in human language, I'd imagine its refrain would sound the same. I was dumbfounded, not because of what Dennis said but because of what I did not say. Not once in my disastrous prepared up, prayed up and versed up "Gospel presentation" did I mention anything about Jesus carrying a cross just for him. I didn't say anything close to it. And so I learned a lesson Paul espoused 2,000-plus years ago: "And when I came to you, brethren, I did not come with superiority of speech or of wisdom, proclaiming to you the testimony of God. For I determined to know nothing among you except Jesus Christ and Him crucified. I was with you in weakness and in fear and in much trembling, and my message and my preaching were not in persuasive words of wisdom, but in demonstration of the Spirit and of power, so that your faith would not rest on the wisdom of men, but on the power of God." (1st Corinthians 2:1-5)

Do you realize what this means for you? It demonstrates how the Kingdom of God does not mandate you hand off perfectly, but that **you do hand off and do so to the best of your ability.**

What happens from that point forward is fittingly out of your hands. Rest assured, if the all-powerful God whom we serve can draw a straight line with a crooked stick, He can likewise draw to Himself whomever He pleases in spite of our deficiencies. No wonder Isaiah 55:11 says, *"So will My word be which goes forth from My mouth; It will not return to Me empty, without accomplishing what I desire, and without succeeding in the matter for which I sent it."* No wonder Romans 9:16 says, "it does not depend on the man who wills or the man who runs, but on God who has mercy."

What, then, can you take away from all this? Be free! Whether others accept or reject the Good News—the baton—is not dependent on you. That means the pressure is off; His summons, however, is still on.

God desires to use you just as you are, wherever you are. Never forget, despite the man and his manner, God's power is perfected through weakness. Much work remains to be done for certain. There's a race to be run and prize to be won. You were designed for the field, not the bleachers.

Please begin making your way out of the stands and onto the track; we welcome you to The Relay!

10

HEBREWS

Hitting the Wall

"Success is to be measured not so much by the position that one has reached in life as by the obstacles which he has overcome while trying to succeed."
—*Booker T. Washington*

You know it when you see it—or rather, hit it. It usually happens around mile 20, give or take a couple of miles. Your pace slows, sometimes considerably. Some runners say that it feels as though their legs had been filled with lead quail shot, like the stomach of Mark Twain's unfortunate jumping frog of Calaveras County. Others can't feel their feet at all. Thought processes become a little fuzzy. ("Mile 22, again? I thought I just passed mile 22!") Muscle coordination goes out the window, and self-doubt casts a deep shadow over the soul.

— "Hitting 'The Wall'" by Sara Latta

This is how Sara Latta described the damage that takes place in long-distance races as two familiar foes collide: the runner and "the wall." Invisible to all but the competitor, the wall's presence is just as tangible to her as the wind at her back. The question is never, "Will I hit it?" but rather, "When will I hit it?" and even more critical, "How will I respond?"

Considering that your Christian life is analogous to a long-distance relay that plays out over the course of time, you must prepare to meet those walls when they come your way. **And they will come:** *"Beloved, do not be surprised at the fiery ordeal among you, which comes upon you for your testing, as though some strange thing were happening to you."* (1st Peter 4:12)

How could you possibly be surprised by this when your own personal walls have been graffitied with words like 'adversity' or 'tribulation,' knowing that neither discriminates, even among Christians? This sobering reality is confirmed by the fact that every Biblical character underwent a significant extent of struggle.

But herein lies one of our faith's greatest beauties: *The Almighty* orders the perfect number of bloodied, battle-hardened runners behind you, beside you and before you—fellow runners empathetic to your plight, urging you forward in your greatest moment of need, saying, "Endure, endure, you have no choice but to press on and endure."

In her book *Stories for the Heart,* author Carole Mayhall recounts a similar example from TV drama called *See How She Runs.*

The story concerns a 40-year-old divorced teacher from Boston who decided to become a jogger and eventually entered the 26-mile Boston Marathon. To finish the race became her goal, and in spite of being harassed, jeered at, and assaulted, she did not lose sight of it. The day of the race came, and she faced her ultimate test. As she ran, huge blisters developed on her feet. She was also hit and injured by a bicycle. And several miles short of the finish line found her utterly exhausted. Yet she kept going. Then, within a few hundred yards of the finish line, late at night when most other runners had either finished or dropped out, she fell and lay flat on her face, too tired to raise her head. But her friends had put up a crude tape across the finish line and began to cheer her on. She lifted her head with great effort, saw the tape, and realized her goal was within sight. With a supreme effort, she got up on her bruised and bleeding feet, and in a burst of energy dredged up from deep inside her courageous heart, she ran the last few yards. She had kept her eyes on the goal and for the joy of finishing, she endured.

The Power of a Cheering Crowd

Not only does the Lord supply our **need** of faithful friends in the here and now, like Carole Mayhall's example above, but for added encouragement, He literally supplies our **want** by helping us envision a massive assembly of ancient martyrs as described in Hebrews 11. He has filled a coliseum to capacity for the sole purpose of cheering you on toward "greater love and good deeds," (Hebrews 10:24) and they are presently doing so, just for you, right now. It's as if these martyrs of the faith have a sixth sense and can identify the very moment when "quit" first enters your mind. As two-time Olympian Todd Williams observed, "Once you're beat mentally, you might as well not even go to the starting line."

Imagine seeing yourself lying motionless up against an invisible but yet very real wall, within earshot of the stadium; you can actually hear the overflow assembly of martyrs' cheers gradually transition into a deafening roar. In unison, their shouts have travelled up, over and beyond those stadium walls. As you pick yourself up and begin to regroup, the *"dense echo of your companions"* (a literal reading of *"a great cloud of witnesses"* in Hebrews 12:1) intersects with your renewed will to press on, morphing into a single word powerful enough to smash any wall: "Endure, endure you have no choice but to press on and endure!"

The imagery above is not fictitious, but represents actual

events as chronicled in Hebrew 12:1: *"Therefore, since we have so great a cloud of witnesses surrounding us, let us also lay aside every encumbrance and the sin which so easily entangles us, and let us run with endurance the race that is set before us."*

What We Do Know about an Unidentified Author

The author who composed the Book of Hebrews has re-mained anonymous since the first century, but we can draw several conclusions about him based on his writings.

First: Undoubtedly, he knew what it meant to hit the wall and endure, which not only allows you to relate but somehow leaves the impression he wrote with your particular circumstances in mind.

Second: He knew full well the power a cheering crowd has to push an athlete to close hard and finish strong. If you go back and read Hebrews, you'll notice how the crowd can-not be seen or heard the first 11 chapters; they only become visible and vocal when competitors need them most—during the final stretch.

Third: Most definitely, he was a runner with unique insights and angles that could only be described by someone who had personally stood on the track looking up into the stands. Notice how he speaks in the third person plural, for instance, in Hebrews 12:1 he says "us" five times.

The Agony of Defeat

In the book of Hebrews, the author's main appeal is to Christians who've previously entered the race of faith and shortly thereafter came to a dead halt as they hit an impene-trable wall of vicious persecution: *"But remember the former days, when, after being enlightened, you endured a great conflict of sufferings, partly by being made a public spectacle through reproaches and tribula-*

tions, and partly by becoming sharers with those who were so treated." (Hebrews 10:32-33)

As numerous believers were poised to drop out, their consensus statement might have read, "Christianity is not what we thought it was." Thankfully, however, the author was in no mood to accept withdrawals but, instead, pressed them deeper into their commitment to Christ and deeper into Christ Himself by telling them to join Him *"outside the camp and bear the reproach He endured."* (Hebrews 13:13 ESV)

Not once did he hint that a Christian's race might be free from agony. He actually did quite the opposite. The Greek word he selected for 'race' was *agon* from which we get the word 'agony.' However, just beyond the *agony,* the author wisely places before the reader the promises of all things better that would one day come, yet with one vital stipulation: You must endure!

> Wilma [Rudolph] didn't get much of a head start in life. A bout with polio left her left leg crooked and her foot twisted inward so she had to wear leg braces. After seven years of painful therapy, she could walk without her braces. At age 12, Wilma tried out for a girls' basketball team but didn't make it. Determined, she practiced with a girlfriend and two boys every day. The next year she made the team. When a college track coach saw her during a game, he talked her into letting him train her as a runner. By age 14, she had outrun the fastest sprinters in the U.S. In 1956, Wilma made the U.S. Olympic team but showed poorly. That bitter disappointment motivated her to work harder for the 1960 Olympics in Rome—and there Wilma Rudolph won three gold medals, the most a woman had ever won. —*Today in the Word,* Moody Bible Institute

Despite the setbacks and hardships, Wilma Rudolph stayed the course; she endured.

What Happens When You Hit the Wall?

Runner Jay Coe reasoned: "Hitting the wall will, over time, and with decent punches, strengthen your knuckles."

Or as Randy Pausch, author of *The Last Lecture,* saw it: "The brick walls are there for a reason. They're not there to keep us out. The brick walls are there to give us a chance to show how badly we want something." Over the course of Pausch's career, he grew to see the walls as presenting new opportunities, which made confronting them head-on all the more bearable.

Starting today, you are presented with the same opportunity to see your walls in an entirely different light. The change of perspective, however, can only begin the moment you sincerely believe that underneath that wall's dreaded wrappings, a gift just might lie inside.

To start that process, let's look at three opportunities these walls can offer: time to look back, to remove from constraint, and to force stillness.

Time to Look Back

Throughout Scripture, the Lord calls and commands us to *"remember."* In other words, to look backward; to not forget all that He has done. In Exodus 13:3 Moses told the people, *"Remember this day in which you went out from Egypt, from the house of slavery; for by a powerful hand the LORD brought you out from this place."*

Sometimes the best way for us to move forward is by first taking a moment to look back. But have you ever noticed how hard it is to run forward while looking backward at the same time? The solution is this: The next time you hit a wall, start looking around for a nearby bench. One will always be there. The Lord kindly places those benches just off your path so that during a time of much-needed respite you'll not only be able to rest but will have the added opportunity to glance over your shoulders to see just how far you've come.

For far too long you have allowed your forward focus to suppress any meaningful attempt at looking back. But as you begin to do so, you will see things you once thought could never be seen: the back sides of impassable walls you were able to scale, walls that are now and forever behind you. The Bible refers to those former barriers as memorials, akin to the national monuments that commemorate historical events.

One such memorial marked the time the entire Israelite Nation stood on the precipice of the Promised Land with one final hurdle blocking their escape. With the Egyptians at their heels, the Jews had no way to go over, go around, much less go through the Jordan River with its overflowing banks. Then came that precise moment when His hand reached far within our notion of time, bringing about a mighty deliverance in such a way as only He could do. After providing a way of escape for His chosen people, The Lord commanded them to build a memorial, saying to them:

> *"When your children ask their fathers in time to come, saying, 'What are these stones?' 22then you shall inform your children, saying, 'Israel crossed this Jordan on dry ground.' 23For the LORD your God dried up the waters of the Jordan before you until you had crossed, just as the LORD your God had done to the Red Sea, which He dried up before us until we had crossed; 24that all the peoples of the earth may know that the hand of the LORD is mighty, so that you may fear the LORD your God forever."* (Joshua 4:21-24)

I refer to those memorials simply as "piles of rocks" and believe God called for them to be built for four key reasons:

1. So those who were there might never forget just how powerfully their God "showed up."

2. As an evangelistic tool so that when younger generations or outsiders inquired, "why are these rocks here?" the older among them might be able to say, "I am pleased you asked. Let me share with you about this amazing time when my Lord showed up."

3. As a reservoir of future faith so that the next time they were hemmed up against an entirely impenetrable wall with no possibility of going over, going around, or much less going through it, they might have faith knowing, "just as He showed up then, I am trusting Him to show up again."

4. The Lord had that pile of rocks set up for you, for all those same reasons listed above. He not only had the events recorded for you but preserved them over thousands of years to speak to you just as He spoke to them: *"God, after He spoke long ago to the fathers in the prophets in many portions and in many ways, in these last days has spoken to us."* (Hebrews 1:1-2)

To make this practical, what would you say the thickest wall is that you are currently up against? Now take a few minutes to look behind you and identify the three or four piles of rocks in your life that stand out most. You can find them right on top of the places where those seemingly indestructible walls once stood. Write down everything you possibly can about them prior to their destruction. Then record in lavish detail, "oh, how great was their fall!"

Returning now to that thickest of walls that currently blocks your path, "oh you of so little faith," how quickly you have forgotten that the Commander of the Lord's army is on your side: "Is not My Word . . . like a mighty hammer that smashes a rock to pieces?" (Jeremiah 23:29, NLT)

The Holy Writings are your lifeline in your great moment of need. Do not refuse them. Look and see just how much encouragement can be found in this one of the Bible's 66 books.

"It was by faith that the people of Israel marched around Jericho for seven days, and the walls came crashing down." (Hebrews 11:30, NLT)

"Therefore, let us draw near with confidence to the throne of grace, so that we may receive mercy and find grace to help in time of need." (Hebrews 4:16)

"Hold fast the confession of our hope without wavering, for He who promised is faithful." (Hebrews 10:23)

"As He Himself has said 'I will never desert you, nor will I forsake you,' so that we confidently say, 'The Lord is my Helper, I will not be afraid!'" (Hebrews 13:5-6)

"Without faith it is impossible to please Him, for he who comes to God must believe that He is and that He is a rewarder of those who seek Him." (Hebrews 11:6)

Please stop reading and pray this very minute. Take a risk of genuine belief trusting that as the Lord showed up back then, He will assuredly show up again.

To Remove from Constraint

Not only do walls give us occasions to look over our shoulders, they force introspection: "Lord, teach me to know You, and to know myself," petitioned Saint Augustine, who was perplexed by how "people travel to wonder at the height of mountains, at the huge waves of the sea, at the long courses of rivers, at the vast compass of the ocean, at the circular motion of the stars; and they pass by themselves without wondering."

Have you ever noticed how overly active many individuals are who are running **away** from Christianity? As long as they are on the go they can hope to avoid that stillness; avoid those quiet moments of introspection when dreaded questions come to mind such as: "Where am I spiritually?" Internal assessments can be enlightening, but only if we carve out enough time to ask ourselves the questions that matter most: *"How many wrongs and sins have I committed? Show me my offense and my sin."* (Job 13:23, NIV)

Walls also free us up to exercise in the process. One fundamental principle in athletics is this: Any athlete wishing to be competitive must develop and adhere to a rigorous exercise routine. Through exercise, hindrances that once bogged a competitor down might be shed away and sloughed off. In a sense, the competitor is then freed up to perform to the best of his or her ability.

The author of Hebrews transferred this principle from the athletic arena into the spiritual one by saying, *"let us also lay aside every encumbrance and the sin which so easily entangles us, and let us run with endurance the race that is set before us."*

More specifically, "lay aside our sin" by definition is to "exercise it," which in turn "moves us out of confinement or restraint." As Mallie Ireland once said, "You can't go very far without taking yourself with you." While true, I would add that through repentance you are able to take less of you than before.

This same principle of removing constraints proved true for Alexander the Great as his army faced imminent defeat as they approached Persia on October 1, 331 BC. It became apparent that the culprit was the loads of plunder his soldiers carried from previous campaigns; it was bogging them down. Knowing that wars are not won with soldiers wielding a sword in one hand and plunder in the other, Alexander ordered all spoils to be piled into a heap and burned. Predictably, the ranks were furious, but as one eyewitness later recorded, the key to their ensuing victory stemmed from the order to shed off the excess weight: "It was as if wings had been given to them—they walked lightly again."

Whenever I hear the expression "removing from constraint," an incredibly convincing story comes to mind that took place in 2016. A group of men from Birmingham, Alabama went on a mission trip with Forgotten Children Ministries in Honduras (founded by Stan Newell, an incredibly gifted preacher from the Mississippi Delta). Another ministry we co-labored with that week was Ben Caleth—an underfunded orphanage for the nation's most severely disabled children.

The environment could not possibly have been more depressing. It might have been half an acre, mostly concrete, enclosed by 8-foot impenetrable walls serving as borders to the home for 20 marginalized children.

One of the boys we met was named Michael. Although he had severe physical deformities, he was able to track along with us in conversation and he was the only one able to do so. His teachers, who had not been paid the previous four months due to a lack of funding, were all too eager to share with us how much English Michael had been learning and how excited he was to try it out on Americans. The anticipation explained why he was unable to sleep the night before.

As my friend Conor pushed Michael around the perimeter of the compound in his wheelchair, Conor discovered that by standing in a particular spot on his tiptoes he could see a breathtaking mountain range in the distance, the peaks of which lay just over the walls. He began to explain to Michael the beauty of what he saw, but he soon realized his English and his descriptors could only go so far with his new-found friend. In his excitement he began to unbuckle Michael from his wheelchair to hoist him up just high enough to see that a whole new world, never before seen, existed beyond those four walls. However, Michael wouldn't budge and began to panic, shaking, almost convulsing, which drew the attention of our entire team. One of his teachers graciously interrupted, and said, "Michael would definitely like to see the mountain range . . . but he is afraid to leave his wheelchair. It's all he has ever known."

"Those walls," those awful 8-foot impenetrable concrete walls served as borders to Michael's lifelong home.

We so desperately wanted to share our long list of reassurances with Michael: "There's an entire new world out there, just beyond those walls; you can trust us, we will not allow you to fall." Those assertions were easily made from where we stood, literally. We knew to tread lightly, however, and therefore, said nothing.

In that context, "to remove from constraint" took on an entirely new meaning. Was his reluctance one of familiarity? Or a fear of putting himself out there, taking a risk, only to be denied by this life once again? Any of those reasons would make sense to those of us on the outside. It would not make sense, however, if any of us on the outside failed to apply those same reasonings and reassurances to the particular barriers or walls against which we currently find ourselves. Michael's story should put anything standing in our way into serious perspective.

To Force Stillness

Whether or not you consciously realize it, an integral part of your design includes a sensor mechanism that lets you know when something within you needs attention, without which you'd be incapable of functioning. While you know full well it's there in one sense, you might pretend you don't in another. To avoid attending to it would be no less futile than to ignore that annoying low-fuel sensor on the dash. Try as you may, that won't make it go away.

Thankfully through a delicate movement of His hand, The Father has intricately woven throughout your entire being a desperate longing for stillness that can only be satiated by rest. As Saint Augustine put it: "You have made us for Yourself, and our hearts are restless until they can find rest in You."

So, what if the walls are there for a reason? Could it be that they are there to prevent you from moving forward, to prevent you from ignoring your intrinsic need for stillness? Whether constructed by The Creator or allowed by Him is beside the point—the fact is that oftentimes those walls are built in to force stillness. And if you would just "cease striving" (Psalm 46:10) long enough, inside the stillness invitations of rest await you. These invitations can always be found:

> *"Come to Me, all who are weary and heavy-laden, and I will give you rest. Take My yoke upon you and learn from Me, for I am gentle and humble in heart, and you will find rest for your souls."* (Matthew 11:28-29)

> *"Thus, says the Lord, 'Stand by the ways and see and ask for the ancient paths, Where the good way is, and walk in it; And you will find rest for your souls.'"* (Jeremiah 6:16)

For a season, therefore, you must rest up and be still. Be obedient to His design. You'll have plenty of time to run in the future—a whole lifetime in fact—but for now, quit staring at that wall, take a seat on that bench and "be diligent to enter that rest!" (Hebrews 4:11)

No Choice but to Endure

One of the greatest examples of what it means to endure took place on October 23, 2014, in Sydney, Australia, as recounted by Dr. David Allen:

> It's a grueling 543.7-mile endurance race from Sydney to Melbourne, Australia—the world's longest and toughest ultra-marathon. In 1983, 150 world-class runners converged on Sydney for the event. On the day of the race, a toothless 61-year-old potato farmer and sheepherder named Cliff Young approached the registration table wearing overalls and galoshes over his work boots. At first, people thought he was there to watch the race, but to their surprise, Cliff Young declared his intention to run and requested a number. Cliff Young had grown up on a farm without the benefit of luxuries like horses and four-wheel drives. When the storms rolled in, Cliff headed out to round up 2000 sheep over a 2000-acre farm. Sometimes he had to run them two or three days to complete the round up. The incredulous staff issued Cliff # 64.
>
> As he mingled with the other runners at the starting line, spectators couldn't believe their eyes. "This must be a joke!" some mused. When the gun went off, bystanders snickered at Cliff, left behind in his galoshes and overalls as the other runners with their sculpted bodies and running gear briskly began the race. Snickers gave way to laughter when Cliff began to run, not like the other runners, but with what could only be described as a leisurely, odd, shuffle.

All of Australia was riveted to the live telecast as they watched the scene unfold. "Someone should stop that crazy old man before he kills himself!" Five days, 15 hours, and 4 minutes later, Cliff Young came shuffling across the finish line in Melbourne, winning the ultra-marathon! He didn't win by a few seconds or even a few minutes. The nearest runner was 9 hours and 56 minutes behind. Australians were stunned at this remarkable yet seemingly impossible victory. How did it happen?

Everyone knew that to run the ultra-marathon, runners would run for 18 hours, then stop and sleep for six hours. This routine was repeated for five punishing days. But no one told Cliff Young. He just shuffled along, day and night, night and day, without stopping to sleep. Cliff broke the previous race record by nine hours and became overnight a national hero.

Interestingly, professional runners began to study and experiment with the odd shuffle that Cliff used in his running. Many long-distance runners have since adopted what has come to be called the "Young shuffle" due to its aerodynamic and energy efficiency.

— "First Person: An ultra-marathon of endurance," by David Allen, Baptist Press

As for the $10,000 prize awarded to the winner? No one bothered to tell Cliff Young about that, either. He was as surprised as any to learn such a prize existed, choosing to give each of the next five runners who placed behind him $2,000 apiece, keeping nothing for himself.

Dr. Allen continues by writing:

Likewise, victory in the Christian life comes through endurance . . . in the short distance race, speed is important. In the long-distance race, endurance is what leads to success.

While Cliff Young achieved a mighty feat of personal endurance, it is Christ Jesus Himself who is the perfect embodiment of endurance and perseverance: *"Who for the joy set before Him endured the cross, despising the shame, and has sat down at the right hand of the throne of God."* (Hebrews 12:2-3)

You see, Christ Himself ran the race . . . He set His face against the popular sin of unbelief and daily lived in patient perseverance, trusting His Father to work everything out for Him. He set the perfect example. As Biblical scholar F.F. Bruce said, "It was sheer faith in God, unsupported by any visible evidence, that carried Him through the taunting, the scourging, the crucifying, and the more bitter agony of rejection, desertion, and dereliction." (Ray C. Stedman, IVP Commentary on Hebrews)

Just knowing all that Christ had to endure for our sakes should give us sufficient reason not to give up: *"For consider Him who has endured such hostility by sinners against Himself, so that you will not grow weary and lose heart."* (Hebrews 12:3)

Three hundred fifty years before the New Testament was written, Aristotle used those exact same expressions "grow weary" and "lose heart" to describe "an athlete who flings himself on the ground panting, relaxation, and collapse after he has surged past the winning post of the race." And no wonder the athlete was victorious! The fact that he collapsed after crossing the finish line proves that he gave everything he had: His tank was empty, and he'd left everything he had on the field.

What, then, are we to make of Hebrews 12:3 when those same expressions are used, only this time prefaced by *"Do not grow weary!"* and *"Do not lose heart!"*—in other words, "do not collapse in panting relaxation after your victory!" In essence, the author is saying, "Not yet; the ultimate victory will only be celebrated once you enter Heaven and stand before your Christ." Until then, the race is set before you; therefore, fix your eyes on Jesus and "endure, endure, you have no choice but to press on and endure."

During the ancient Olympic Games, the Athenians had a noteworthy race where each runner carried a lighted torch. The objective was not to finish first but to finish with one's torch still lit—a fitting analogy for the Christian life.

A parallel to those races of lit torches can be found in Hebrews 13:7, a verse foundational to the overarching purpose of Hebrews: *"Remember those who led you, who spoke the word of God to you; and considering the result of their conduct, imitate their faith."*

If imitation is the greatest form of flattery, then by all means, flatter your spiritual forefathers by imitating their faith: Keep running The Relay and keep your torch lit!

THE PODIUM

Forgetting What Lies Behind and
Reaching for What Lies Ahead

"In the dust of defeat as well as the laurels of victory there is a glory to be found if one has done his best." —*Eric Liddell*

Monday, April 19, Patriot's Day, broke warm and blue over Boston, perfect for just about anything except running 26.2 miles. . . .

They had nothing in common. One was a humble farm boy from Minnesota. The other was the most electrifying distance runner of his time. In 1982, they battled stride for stride for more than two hours in the most thrilling Boston Marathon ever run. Then the drama really began.

That is how writer John Brant begins his fascinating article in *Runner's World* magazine, "Duel in the Sun," which catalogued the intermingling paths of Dick Beardsley and Alberto Salazar, two of the world's most storied runners. Salazar staggered across the line first in 2:08:51, Beardsley in 2:08:53, less than 2 seconds separating the two. Both broke what was then the American record, and the times still stand as the sixth and seventh fastest U.S. performances ever. It would take many years for each man independent of the other to discover in a sense there has to be more, much more. Their stories bring to mind another Liddell quote: "Many of us are missing something in life because we are after the second best."

The reason I chose to close out *The Relay* on their respective journeys is that each best mirrors what this book is all about. Here were two men who built their athletic careers as individual athletes, marathoners who relied exclusively on self to achieve the task at hand. But over time they transitioned, maybe even graduated, into types of long-distance relay runners who furthered a greater cause. Analogous to the classic introduction to ABC's *Wide World of Sports*, Salazar's transition seemingly began after the thrill of victory; Beardsley's after the agony of defeat. The Boston Marathon brought them fame; adversity brought them low; passing the baton to others brought them meaning.

With Beardsley, a farming accident eventually led to his struggles deep within the tangled maze of addiction. From "Duel in the Sun":

> Somehow, the tractor engine died. Beardsley pulled his crushed leg out of the machine and crawled out to the yard, where Mary finally found him. Beardsley was relatively lucky; power take-off accidents kill more farmers than they maim. He came away with a punctured lung, a

fractured right wrist, broken ribs, a severe concussion, broken vertebrae, a mangled leg, and a monkey on his back.

That first rush of Demerol in the hospital was unlike anything the straight arrow, teetotaling Beardsley had ever experienced. He rocketed into another world—one without stress or strain or worry. It was so wonderful that if some higher power told him that he could go back, avoid the accident, but never take Demerol, Beardsley wouldn't hesitate—he would turn down the offer flat.

His subsequent recovery and treatment wouldn't come without a fight, but he did come out with a renewed sense of passing his triumphs forward, saying: "I really feel that God let me get so close to death and then said 'Ok enough is enough, I'm going to get you better and I want you to share your journey to help others."

In the case of Salazar, nobody would guess that a first-place finish felt like second best. Again, quoting Brant's *Runner's World* article:

In the weeks and months following the 1982 Boston Marathon, Alberto Salazar's decline was so gradual that it barely seemed like a decline at all . . . in 1990 he was interviewed by a local priest. At long last, the former champion acknowledged his pain and emptiness. He told the priest he was once presented with a wreath of genuine green laurels after winning a marathon. "My father took it with him and preserved it as a memento in a safe place," he said. "Several months later, this beautiful wreath, which marked a great victory, had lost its entire beauty. For sport is not simply a discipline," Salazar continued. "Sport can become a compulsion, another god. So long as one depends on it, he forgets everything else. If he loses this god, he has nothing else.

Years later he was hired on by an athletic shoe company "as a kind of coach-at-large, chartered to deliver that most endangered of species—The Great American Distance Runner—from the brink of extinction." Ironically, the athletic shoe company's name in Greek means "victory," more famously known as Nike. But as you can tell by the quote below, Salazar's ideals were much higher than selling shoes.

> "Whatever we accomplish in life, if it's solely for our own good, then it doesn't mean that much. The things you do that affect others in a positive way are the ones that count. Whatever facet of life you're in, God has given you a gift; do the best you can with that gift."

In an email to *Runner's World*, Salazar would say of his archrival: "Dick has impressed me because he's gone through some hard times, but because of his faith in God he has used those experiences to become a better person and to help others. He has been an inspiration to me in that regard." To this day, the former rivals stay in touch and share a common spirituality.

Hardship's tendency, in whatever form it may take, can turn even the plushest laurel's greenery into a bleak wintry gray, as the "Duel in the Sun" heroes can assuredly relate. Adversity, trial, pain are all too eager and happy to facilitate internal dialogue for those of us who are its familiar foes: questions of self-doubt and second guessing. "Am I making a difference?" "Does what I'm doing really matter?" "Is this all there is? There has to be more . . . much more."

The most important thing is how we respond to those questions, the answers to which should prod us to seek out wreaths of a more meaningful sort; those loftier mementos with eternal significance awarded for victories in life that really matter most, such as trophies that are "imperishable and undefiled and will not fade away, reserved in heaven for you"

(1st Peter 1:4), but are also celebrated in community rather than individually— *"in the future there is in the future there is laid up for me the crown of righteousness, which the Lord, the righteous Judge, will award to me on that day; and not only to me, but also to all who have loved His appearing."* (2nd Timothy 4:8)

Wreaths of a More Meaningful Sort

"It has been a wonderful experience to compete in the Olympic Games and to bring home a gold medal. But since I have been a young lad, I have had my eyes on a different prize. You see, each one of us is in a greater race than any I have run in Paris, and this race ends when God gives out the medals." —Eric Liddell

If I could give a prize for one story in real time that best exemplifies what *The Relay* is all about, I'd look no further than my own home. It revolves around my youngest son Georgie, who happens to be a runner—fast as a jackrabbit, as my mother would say. Few highlights in a dad's life could surpass cheering his child on in competition or relishing the moment he or she ascends the podium to be awarded a top prize. When Georgie won State in junior high hurdles in 2014, it was a fine individual achievement, no doubt. Jill and I celebrated as much as any in the Birmingham Metroplex. The medal is still on display at home.

And yet our proudest moment of him bar none is currently on display at the high school he attends. You see, since junior high, Georgie ran up against his own set of hurdles— some anxiety and depression, obstacles invisible to his peers but easily identifiable by us, his parents. He came by it honestly, as I've experienced those troubles myself. My top two prayers over the last 25 years might be one indication: "Lord, please let my children determine to nothing among themselves, except Christ and Him crucified. Lord, please allow my depression and anxiety to pass over my children." That's the exact order, every time.

Rarely, if ever, will you hear anyone admit in public, "I'm struggling in the here and now." The tendency, especially in the Deep South, is to vaguely share obstacles from the distant past that have since been easily cleared "thanks to the Lord, of course. His grace is sufficient."

Believe me, I love an uplifting, *"we are more than conquerors through Him who loved us"* (Romans 8:37) story as much as any—the Bible is chock full of them for a reason. They have their time and place. What most of us need, more than anything else, is to occasionally hear from a brave soul gutsy enough to put his or her real self out in front of us and share what is truly going on, whether good, bad or ugly.

When my son Georgie stepped up to address his fellow students as the president of student government, he did so from a position of weakness rather than strength, sharing some of the highs and lows of what's he's been through. No doubt it was music to the ears of fellow strugglers—which, truthfully, includes all of us to one degree or another. In closing, he assured them, "You're not alone because I know there are at least two of us out there. If I'm only speaking to one person in this room, I'm telling you there is help out there; just as it was for me." What he did made a difference because all those students who assumed they were the "one person in the room" started to ease out of the shadows. And there are a lot of them.

What Georgie did gives hope. It gives us a reason to feel less isolated. I've never been more proud!

Yes, God's grace is sufficient on top of the podium. We all get that. But you know what? It's nice to be reminded by someone like my son that it's just as sufficient in the depths of the pit. That is ministry. That is the "greater race" Liddell referenced above. That is the Relay.

And I'm telling you, that is ministry as much as the finest sermon from any pulpit I've ever heard.

"I have no greater joy than this, to hear of my children walking in the truth." —3 John 1:4

Running for More

In ancient Rome, the citizenry was accustomed to the influx of foreign athletes descending on their city every three to four years. Each had completed 10 months of rigorous training *(gymnazo)*, followed by 30 days of exercises at the gymnasium, in hopes of satisfying the appointed officers just to compete in any of the Olympic Games. It was common knowledge then as now: Competitions might be lost in the gym, but only won on the field.

Paul, for one, took advantage of that backdrop by applying the same Greek word to spiritual training, which is *gymnazo*, like 'gymnasium,' which "conveys acquiring proficiency through practice—regular exercise with graduated resistance." (HELPS Word Studies definition) Paul coached his young mentee Timothy by advising him *"train (gymnazo) yourself for the purpose of Godliness"* (1st Timothy 4:7), knowing first hand how treacherous the anti-Christian resistance ahead would become. It was paramount for Timothy to strive (agónizomai or 'agonize') prior to setting out so his future progress would not be hindered. Paul instructed him to *"take pains with these things; be absorbed in them, so that your progress will be evident to all."* (1st Timothy 4:15) 'Progress' was a loaded term in the first century, meaning "to chop down whatever gets in your way," such as a tree or stump, i.e., advancement by any means necessary.

Training to a degree is useful but limited unless applied. Timothy was not allowed to rest on his laurels from the gym. At some point the training regimen, Paul laid out for him led out the door: *"pay close attention to yourself ("apply yourself"* *in Greek) and to your teaching; persevere in these things, for as you do* *this ("as you carry this out, as you accomplish this") you will ensure* *salvation both for yourself and for those who hear you."* (1st Timothy 4:16) The devil's trick has always been to convince the faithful that whatever godly endeavor we put our hand to, there'll be plenty of time to tend to it down the road; i.e., "not today, maybe tomorrow."

But life is uncertain, and now is the best time for you to make continual forward progress in spiritual matters.

In death as in life, Saint Paul best typifies what *The Relay* is all about, probably more than any other. If you set out to emulate a single runner from the crowded field of those we've studied thus far, he would top the list. His philosophy of accomplishment would be today's anomaly, especially when it comes to competition. He would have balked at the catchphrase, "It's not whether you win or lose; it's how you play the game." Participation trophies would seem bizarre at best, outright unhealthy at worst. If, as Michelangelo said, "the greater danger for most of us lies not in setting our aim too high and falling short; but in setting our aim too low and achieving our mark," then imminent danger in this respect was never a threat . . . Paul's sights were set high.

Reflecting on his personal race, he put it this way: *"not that I* *have already obtained it or have already become perfect, but I press on so* *that I may lay hold of that for which also I was laid hold of by Christ* *Jesus. Brethren, I do not regard myself as having laid hold of it yet; but* *one thing I do: forgetting what lies behind and reaching forward to what* *lies ahead, I press on toward the goal for the prize of the upward call* *of God in Christ Jesus!"* (Philippians 3:12-14) Likewise, antislavery crusader and African missionary David Livingstone determined to "open up Africa or perish." In a letter home to the London Missionary Society, he was glad to be at their disposal to go anywhere in Africa, "provided it be forward!"

That is Paul's faith race in one word: Forward! His starting line began on an obscure Damascus road when first apprehended by Christ and continued up until the final bell lap's ring in a Roman jail, ever abiding in a relentless pursuit of his Messiah. If we are to emulate Paul—and he clearly said that we should—we must first peer into the mind of the man and his mission determining what motivated him to press on with such unbridled intensity for the better part of 30 years. Even "unbridled intensity" isn't forceful enough to express his intent because the word he chose for "pressing on" was *dioko*, used to depict the final strides of a race in which Olympians strained every sinew in their entire bodies forward stretching out to apprehend the prize. *Dioko* also referred to a fierce warrior "aggressively hunting down in order to apprehend" his prey. So what was Paul after?

The highest ideal for Paul running for the King's glory was to win, which he did, and while so doing, won multitudes in the process, who, in turn, were to win even more and more, that all might be awarded the ultimate prize.

In other words, a perpetual, continual forwarding of the baton as described in 2nd Timothy 2:2: *"The things which you have heard from me in the presence of many witnesses, entrust these to faithful men who will be able to teach others also."*

Our calling is to do no less.

The only semblance of Paul's slowdown came in the form of failing health and four walls imprisoning him as a criminal, or, as he explained: *"for I am already being poured out as a drink offering, and the time of my departure has come"* which required no interpretation. To depart was a common euphemism for death, meaning to "loosen a ship from its moorings" or to "break camp," the latter being especially poignant for a man who earned his living as a tentmaker such as Paul. As the curtains were closing in on him within that cold, damp cell, his last changeover was taking place.

Theologian Gordon Fee put it this way: "Here we have a changing of the guard, the word of a dying man to his heir apparent. To use the athletic metaphor, it is the passing of the baton."

Hurrying to finalize a last will and testament of sorts, Paul's postscript reads, *"I solemnly charge you in the presence of God and of Christ Jesus, who is to judge the living and the dead, and by His appearing and His kingdom: preach the Word..."* (2nd Timothy 4:1-2) It's as if we can imagine him, baton (the Word of God) in hand, feebly uttering: "Young Timothy, much work remains to be done. If you don't get anything else from my Christ-consumed life, I beg you to secure this simple command: Preach the Word! Timothy, you must pass it forward. Preach the Word! There's a race not only to be run, there's a race to be won."

What if, regardless of your current stage or station of faith, you, like the Apostle Paul, or Dick Beardsley, or Alberto Salazar, or my son George, were called up to start running for more—He always calls for more—as if all that's gone before has trained you for what's in store? More of an impact? More reach? More meaning? More of what in life matters most?

What if you were "chartered to help deliver that most endangered of species" similar to Salazar, except, in this case, Christians were the ones on "the brink of extinction?" Recall the quote from the first chapter: "Christianity is never more than one generation away from extinction." Could ours be the generation to once again *"turn the entire world upside down,"* (Acts 17:6) as the Thessalonians jeered in protest against the Gospel's spread in their region over 2,000 years ago?

If history repeats itself, and clearly it does, the same nation that birthed a first Great Awakening and a second Great Awakening is overdue for its third. Enough already with the preparations; I see no shortage of Christians preparing to forward their faith, but acting on it seems to be an entirely different matter.

You, women of God and men of God, must start chasing after the souls of your fellow women and men with as much unbridled intensity as with all the other things of this world you're so desperately running after.

In Charles Spurgeon's strong words: "It is not a new person or a new plan, but the life of God in you that the church needs. Let us ask God for it! Perhaps God is ready to shake the world at its very foundations. Perhaps even now, He is about to pour forth a mighty influence upon His people, which shall make the church in this age as vital as it ever was in any age that has passed."

"It takes a dream to get started, desire to keep going, and determination to finish." —Eddie Harris Jr.

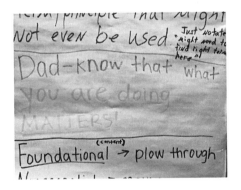

This book's completion was never more in doubt than a year before its publication. To say I've never been bombarded by more waves of discouragement from every side simultaneously is no understatement; I'd rank it the most discouraging season in my life.

In fact, when my car overheated out in the country late one Friday night for the third time in 24 hours, and I was unable to call for a tow because my phone was broken, and even if I could have, all my credit cards were locked up from being hacked, not to mention a whopping unexpected bill on my desk at work, comparatively speaking, it was a minor first-world inconvenience at worst—the least of my worries in the grand scheme of other troubles.

For some reason, all the external junk brought to the surface months' worth of self doubt and hard-core second-guessing, all centering around this book. The sole journal entry for that week said it all: "All this [writing] is a complete waste of time, it doesn't matter whatsoever." Yes, I'll confess, I had conquered the "dream to get started" part of Harris' quote above, but the "desire" and "determination" pieces had all but disappeared, and I mean it.

I did manage to get my car up and running after some tinkering, at least long enough to make a quick stop at my office to pick up that whopping unexpected bill before heading home. It was well past midnight, and since I was the only one in the building, I have no idea why I shut my door behind me for all of three seconds. I never do that, but that night I was glad I did because as I turned to leave, a poster normally hidden behind my door came into full view. Apparently my daughter Sydney felt an overwhelming prodding come over her to write me a word of encouragement earlier that day: "Dad—know that what you are doing MATTERS!"

Unbeknownst to her then (she's not even aware of it until now), I had previously offered up a day's worth of what I call "empty-handed prayers"— those very few and far between moments of complete surrender, when everything I am and all that I have was on His table—and He knew it because He knows me intimately. "Lord, all I have is on Your table. If there is anything in my life that is keeping my affections away from You, do with it what you may. Please make it painfully obvious what You would have me do. It would be really nice to hear from You sooner than later."

I was convinced He would take nothing less than what I

had labored over for so long, actually for more years, away from other priorities, than I'd really prefer to admit. *The Relay* was my decades-long dream in the making, the hardest effort of my life, in fact. I had put my hand to the plow with no intention of ever turning back, but if that was what He wanted me to offer up to His altar, I would. I'm not sure I could describe how terribly saddened I was at the thought of walking away, not to mention how terribly confused. But something had to give. I was worn out.

It's not possible for me to describe exactly what Sydney's scribbled note did for me. There's no reason to belabor the point. Just suffice it to say it made all the difference in such a way I cannot explain. They were the exact right words I needed to hear at the exact right moment. Those eight words gave me all the confidence I needed to proceed. In hindsight, it seems as if The Lord put a test before me, waiting until I placed everything on the altar before giving any confirmation.

But that's not all. For added measure, a reconfirmation was on its way. In a movement only The Divine could orchestrate with His impeccable timing, we were invited to dinner the next night at our friends Will and Ammie Akin's house. As we were getting up to leave after a nice meal and fellowship, Ammie kept inquiring—insisting, really, as if a radar in her spirit could not be turned off— "so George, I really want to know, tell me about your week." Sensing she was genuinely interested, I spared few details, only leaving out the part about Sydney's kind message.

She asked, "Out of curiosity, what chapter have you been working on these last few months?"

"That's easy," I said. "Hebrews: Hitting the Wall. It's about adversity and tribulation, obstacles that block our paths seemingly impossible to clear, how we must get up, regroup and run the race that is set before us with endurance.

Why do you ask?"

Ammie looked me squarely in the face in an unabashed way demanded by the moment and said, "Listen to me, this is not a coincidence. Do you realize the chapter you're writing will make a difference in people's lives who need to hear it? What you are doing matters. It matters a lot, and satan knows it. He's throwing everything he can at you to prevent you from proceeding."

Rising up from her chair as if ascending a pulpit to drive home her closing remark, she said, "You rebuke him in Jesus' Holy Name and demand, 'get thee behind me satan!'"

G. K. Chesterton once wrote: "All men matter. You matter. I matter. It's the hardest thing in theology to believe." I'd like to believe this book will matter, that it will make a difference for some. If for no other reason than to assist Christian sprinters and marathoners to become relay runners for the long haul.

Our world needs the baton, which is the Word of God, now more than ever, and we all know that. We really do. The Lord chose to use you and me to pass it forward, so in a real sense, the baton is in our hands. Once you start passing it and start upping your spiritual game, get ready: You'll find difficulties just ahead. To suggest otherwise would be neither Biblical nor right.

> "Growth is painful. Change is painful. But nothing is as painful as staying stuck somewhere you don't belong."
>
> —author Mandy Hale

Take heart and know that many difficulties you face won't be because you're doing something wrong, but simply because you'll be doing what is right, what matters.

So go ahead and get started. There's a race not only to be run; there's a race to be won!

About the Author

In the summer of 1995, George Shamblin left a successful career in pharmaceutical sales, and a year-end bonus large enough to pay for three years of tuition, to enroll at Reformed Theological Seminary in Jackson, MS. Though he experienced more than his share of challenges and setbacks over the next 25 years, it's a decision he's never regretted.

Since 2012, Shamblin has served as a pastor with The Center For Executive Leadership in Birmingham, Alabama — where he teaches Bible Studies, disciples others at various stages of spiritual growth, and maintains an active role in leading overseas mission trips. Also an adjunct professor at Birmingham Theological Seminary, Shamblin published his first book, *The Relay*, in 2020.

An avid outdoorsman, as well as Master Gardener, George and his wife of 27 years, Jill, have four children — Sydney, Bailey, Miller, and George Jr.

 @TheRelaybyGSham    @TheRelaybyGSham

 @TheRelaybyGSham